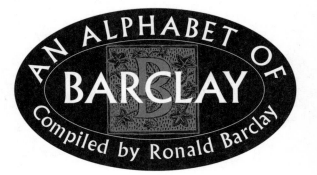

AN ALPHABET OF BARCLAY

Compiled by Ronald Barclay

SAINT ANDREW PRESS

Edinburgh

First published in 1999 by
SAINT ANDREW PRESS
BOARD of COMMUNICATION
CHURCH of SCOTLAND
121 George Street, Edinburgh EH2 4YN

Copyright © W J Ronald Barclay 1999

ISBN 0 7152 0692 3

British Library Cataloguing in Publication Data
A catalogue record for this book
is available from the British Library.

ISBN 0715206923

Cover design by Mark Blackadder.
Cover and internal illustrations by Sheila Cant.
Typeset in 10/13 pt Bembo.
Printed and **bound** by Redwood Books

CONTENTS

INTRODUCTION

by Ronald Barclay

ON the 5th December 1907 my father, William Barclay, was born in Wick, Caithness in North Scotland. He never really knew Wick and his life in the north did not have any noticeable effect on his writings. What did leave its mark on him was the age of his father, 41, and his mother, 38. Willie Barclay grew up in a well-respected home with the love and care of two mature and contented people. This happy and stress-free childhood undoubtedly made him the man he was.

It is interesting to note that my father's ancestors on the Barclay side came from Lochgoilhead and it is part of the oral tradition of the oldest inhabitants of that town that the Barclays of days gone by were great singers and loved music. It has often been a source of puzzlement to me why my father was so interested in music. His own singing voice was just bearable and many of his former students who were members of his College Choir have told me that his musical talents were based more on enthusiasm than skill! But the love of music was certainly there, inherited from these Lochgoilhead ancestors who loved to sing long ago.

To this day two memorials remain in Lochgoilhead: the traces of Barclay's jetty, built by Willie's grandfather; and the Barclay tombstone in the Church of the Three Holy Brethren.

We next find mention of the Barclays at Fort William in the census return for 1861. On 7th July 1864 my grandfather, William Dugald Barclay, was born. His chosen career was banking. In 1891 he was a teller in Fort William; in 1905 he was appointed manager in Wick. On 26th July 1906 he married my grandmother, Barbara McLeish (despite opposition from her parents who did not consider 'WDB' good enough for their daughter). Their happiness was complete when my father was born in December of the following year.

My father once said: 'Whatever I have done in life, it is because I stood on the shoulders of my parents.' Willie had a privileged and happy childhood for which he never ceased to be grateful. I have no doubt at all that the happy childhood experienced by my sister and myself reflected my father's childhood happiness and security.

Willie Barclay was indeed a happy, secure, optimistic person. Son of a successful father and a gifted, graceful mother, his outlook on life was permanently formed by his early experience of family life. From his father he inherited a passion for literature, the aim to be an active participant in the Church and a desire to win souls for Christ. From his mother he inherited a peace, calmness and graciousness of spirit which he never lost, even in the dark days that were to befall him.

'My mother was a saint ... above all she was kind ... lovely in body and spirit, good all through,' he once said. It is not difficult to see why William Barclay became the talented, kind, generous man he was, with parents like that.

Recently I visited Kilmallie Cemetery in Corpach near Fort William, the spot where my father's parents are buried, the grave marked by a simple Celtic cross. As I looked out at Loch Linnhe I could well understand the effect of the peace with which the whole area is filled and I can imagine my father and his parents spending happy days on holiday there during his childhood years, basking in an atmosphere of calm and tranquillity in this beautiful countryside.

At the age of five my father arrived in Motherwell, a town in central Scotland, quite different from the peace and quiet of Wick and his holidays in Fort William. His father was appointed bank manager there and a new life awaited my father. Motherwell was the town which he eventually considered to be his home and my sister and I were rarely taken to Fort William and never to Wick in our childhood.

Willie's health, which in later years was excellent, was at that time quite poor and in 1913 he suffered from a severe attack of scarlet fever which affected his hearing. It is a supreme irony that one of Scotland's outstanding communicators was almost stone deaf. Our family have many memories of my father's deafness — and the tricks he used to play on us! He would sit there, when he felt he needed peace from all our chatter and nonsense, with the volume of his hearing aid turned down and a contented smile on his face. The problem was that you never knew whether the volume was up or down, and we had many a hilarious time with crazy conversations that belonged more to the realms of 'The Goon Show' or 'Monty Python'!

My father's deafness was only the first of a remarkable series of misfortunes which befell him during his life. I have no doubt that his greatest strength was his ability to put himself in the shoes of fellow sufferers. The suffering which followed him relentlessly made him direct his ministry to those who needed help.

In Motherwell, Willie attended Dalziel High School, a school with an excellent academic and sporting tradition. My father entered both arenas with enthusiasm and outstanding success. Even when I was in my late teens, he could beat me at tennis and flight the ball well past my bat at cricket.

My grandfather continued to lead a full, active life. In May 1925 he was appointed Justice of the Peace for the County of Lanark. My father's relationship with his parents at this time was a strange mixture. An only child of successful and publicly acclaimed parents, living in a house full of love and caring, but often not on the same wavelength as his parents, my father must have felt the tension. Despite his outward appearance of total strength and conviction, my father was a very vulnerable person and I have strong memories of moments when he wanted to be told that what he was doing was right and when he needed encouragement and support.

During the summer of 1920, Willie decided to become a minister and from that moment on he never looked back from that call from God. In October 1925, he started his chosen course of Latin and Greek at the University of Glasgow and in 1929 he graduated Master of Arts with first class honours. He gained his Bachelor of Divinity with distinction in 1932 and a long and distinguished career stretched before him.

But then the suffering, which followed him so often in his life, struck again. Just before he was licensed to be a minister in the Church of Scotland, his mother died a painful death from cancer of the spine. My father used to tell how his father said to him at that tragic moment, 'Your preaching will have a new note in it now'.

I never knew my grandmother – she died before I was born – but I know from the rare moments when my father talked to us about her that she had a formative and lasting influence on him.

My father had a strange relationship with my grandfather. He held him in great love, admiration and respect, but there seems to be no doubt that they argued frequently! My grandfather's strict theological views must have been the perfect field for lively discussion and sometimes heated argument. Indeed my father's entry in *Who's Who* under 'hobbies' states: 'Music and arguments'!

All my father's references to my grandmother indicate that he considered her to be a saint. His first major book, Acts – the first volume in the *Daily Study Bible Readings* – has this dedication:

> *In grateful memory of*
> *W.D.B. and B.L.B.*
> *From whose lips I first heard*
> *The Name of Jesus*
> *And in whose lives*
> *I first saw Him.*

Another formative influence on my father was Professor Bultmann of the University of Marburg in Germany, under whom my father studied before taking up his first Church of Scotland charge. Bultmann's modern approach to New Testament studies was the starting point for my father's delight in exploring the background to the life of Jesus and the New Testament.

My father's first church – Trinity Church, Renfrew on the Clydeside – was no easy charge. It had not managed to keep a minister for more than four years. Again and again, in later life, he would refer to those 14 years in Renfrew. He learned how to communicate with people in his time there. He took further the skills of argument and debate which he had practised with his father, and he never failed to give Trinity Church full recognition for the role it played in making him the man he became.

In particular, he loved to tell the story of the old lady whom he was visiting and who was confined to bed.

'Mr Barclay,' she said, 'when you are sitting here beside me I can understand every word you say. When you're up in that pulpit I don't know what you're going on about!'

He took those words to heart. Many years later his 'Plain Man' series showed he had not forgotten that his first duty was to make the great truths of the Bible and, in particular, the New Testament, relevant and meaningful to the 'ordinary man and his wife'.

My father married my mother on the 30th June 1933. When he married her, he took on her four sisters and my grandmother, who was also a minister's wife in a small Ayrshire village which she ran most efficiently and competently! My poor father never fully recovered from this female onslaught and the interesting result to note is the very male-orientated character of much of his writing.

Where nowadays we would use expressions like 'people' or 'persons', 'we' or 'they', for example, my father would, without fail, use 'man', 'men', and so on, in *all* of his works! How he would have coped with our present world of inclusive language is an interesting thought. I often quote a poem which my father loved to quote:

Lord on whom all love depends,
Let us make and keep good friends.
Bless me also with the patience
To endure my wife's relations.

In June 1937 my sister, Barbara, was born. I always have great pleasure remembering those happy days in Renfrew when the world seemed to stand still and all was well.

My father's great love in those early Renfrew days was for the young people and it was his main aim to make Jesus' message meaningful for them. Many of his books were originally written for Bible Class, Sunday School or Boys Brigade. All these organisations thrived in Trinity Church and the wider Church benefited when he became Convener of the Youth Committee of the Church of Scotland.

William's preaching at that time has been described as biblically based and eloquent, with a richness of detail drawn from his incredible memory, full of logic and clarity and a fine devotional spirit. He was certainly an exacting taskmaster on himself. He took great pride in sticking rigidly to the time allocated to him for his sermons, addresses and talks.

He loved to tell this story of two old men in church. One cannot cope with the long-winded, rambling sermon and he falls asleep. Suddenly he wakes up and asks his neighbour: 'Has he no finished yet?' Back comes the answer: 'Aye, he's finished, but he canna stop!'

In 1939, at a moment of despair for our nation, my father issued his own statement of faith:

I believe in God. I believe in Jesus. I believe in the Holy Spirit. I believe in Christian hope. I believe in the Holy Scriptures. I believe in the Church. I believe in the life of the Christian as an individual. I believe in the life of the Christian as a member of the community.

With war just round the corner it was a courageous declaration of faith.

My father was not fit for Army Service because of his deafness, but he and my mother played their part in Renfrew. I remember those days well. The Blitz became so bad that my sister and I, along with my mother, had to be evacuated to Dundonald to stay with my grandparents, but my father stayed on in Renfrew through the terrible days of the Clydebank Blitz.

On the 13th October 1946 my father announced his resignation from Trinity Church to begin a long and distinguished career at the University of Glasgow, first as a lecturer in New Testament Language and Literature and later as Professor of Divinity and Biblical Criticism. He often described himself as a 'theological middleman' and he would not have claimed to be a great scholar. His skill lay in interpreting the works of great scholars and passing the information on in non-technical language to ordinary people.

He continued to write for the *Scottish Sunday School Teacher* magazine. He produced materials for day schools. He wrote for ministers in the *British Weekly* and *Expository Times*. He had a constant round of engagements, conferences, talks, preaching, even 'Immortal Memories' at Burns Suppers!

However, due to the ill health of his professor he was heavily committed to a very full lecturing programme. It was a time-consuming, hectic round of commitments, but he never complained and very rarely turned down any request for him to talk at a function. I have clear memories of driving into Central Station in Glasgow to collect him off the train and take him home. And, of course, I always took Rusty, his beloved Stafford-shire Bull Terrier, with me! Many is the moral that my father drew from the behaviour of Rusty!

I also have many happy memories of holidays spent with my parents and sister in places like Dunbar, North Berwick and Lunan Bay, and also in Eastbourne where my father combined a holiday with taking the services in a local church. Later my wife and I went with our children and my parents and sister to Elie and Arbroath on the East coast of Scotland, great favourites of my father's.

Despite the colossal pressure on him, my father still had time for us. He was a most generous and loving husband, father and grandfather. I like to think of him in terms of the words of one of his favourite poems by Kagawa, the Japanese Christian:

I read in a book
About a man called Christ
Who went about
Doing good.
It is very disconcerting
To me
That I am so easily
Satisfied
With just
Going about.

My father was a man who was never satisfied with 'just going about'. Many books appeared from his pen in the early 1950s: *Ambassador for Christ,* his life of St Paul; *And Jesus said*, a hand-book for the Parables; *And He had Compassion on Them*, his guide to the Miracles.

It was astonishing how acceptable his books were to a great variety of people and opinions. The Salvation Army used some of his books in its training classes. Ministers, priests, ordinary lay people, all came to appreciate his way of making the mysteries of the New Testament come alive and take on meaning.

As already mentioned, many of his books were originally written for young people, but some of these handbooks became fascinating material for an older readership than they were intended for.

'My one aim has been to make the picture of Jesus live again,' he said. His intention was 'to make the life and words of Jesus live against their contemporary background and, above all, to make them relevant for today'.

One of his favourite challenges was: 'If you want to keep alive, keep learning!' I remember him telling us how horrified he was to find some of the textbooks his students had been using for his courses in second-hand bookshops after the course was over. He could not understand how anyone could sell the tools of the trade and he never failed to claim that 'to think is a necessity of the Christian life' and that by reading and understanding the New Testament we can come closer to our Master.

There is an ironic twist to his most famous publication of all – the *Daily Study Bible*. When he started this remarkable series of interpretations of the books of the New Testament in 1953, he was asked to fill in for someone who was unable to do the first volume of the Bible readings and notes due to illness. What was meant to be a temporary answer to an immediate problem became a world-famous series of commentaries on the New Testament.

The series was completed between 1953 and 1959 and today there are translations in Russian, German, Norwegian, Danish, Indonesian, and many more. Millions of copies of the 'DSB', as it has come to be known as, have found their way into homes all over the world. The simplicity of style, the mastery of the art of bringing the words of the New Testament to both the man and woman in the pew, and to the unchurched masses, have made this work unique. It is an outstanding memorial to my father and to his cherished aim to give ordinary people the opportunity to gain a better understanding of the New Testament.

On the 6th July 1956, the conferring of a Doctor of Divinity degree by the University of Edinburgh was a high point in my father's life. He suffered all his life from lingering doubts that he was not accepted by his fellow academics. Despite protestations that he did not mind the unspoken but evident disapproval and the accusations that his writings were too 'popular' and not scholarly enough, my father was vulnerable to feelings of not being an academic and not being on a par with his fellow scholars. The degree from Edinburgh helped him to see that at least part of the academic world *did* appreciate his efforts to bring Jesus to the people.

At this moment of happiness and pleasure that he had been recognised at last, suffering struck again. My sister, Barbara, was drowned in a tragic boating accident on the 9th August in Northern Ireland, one short month after my father reached his academic pinnacle.

'The greatest heroism of all,' he said, 'is to keep going .... This is only the end of one chapter: it is not the end of the book.'

I once gave a talk on my father and his books in the Southside of Glasgow and a man came up to me afterwards and told me that my father had quoted the following poem in his sermon in an Edinburgh church on the Sunday after my sister's death:

Shall I wear mourning for my soldier dead
I – a believer? Give me red,
Or give me royal purple for the King
At whose royal court my love is visiting.
Dress me in green for growth, for life made new,
For skies his dear feet march, dress me in blue,
In white for his white soul; robe me in gold
For all the pride that his new rank shall hold.
In earth's dim gardens blooms no hue too bright
To dress me for my love who walks in light.

The tragedy of my sister's death must have created as much grief as any man could bear, but worse was to come. After my father's death on the 24th January 1978 we found a letter in his jacket pocket, a letter which he had received after my sister's death and which we knew about at the time, although we did not know that he had been carrying it about with him all those years. The letter ran:

> *Dear Dr Barclay,*
> *I know why God killed your daughter. It was to save her*
> *from being corrupted by your heresies.*
>
> *signed: A Christian*

Had the letter been signed, my father would have written to the person concerned, not in anger, but in an attempt to discuss the problem. I have no doubt that my father upset many people. He often put his views in a forceful and determined way, which inevitably disturbed those who did not agree with him – but he did not deserve the vicious attack which that letter contained.

A year after my sister's death, my mother and father adopted Jane, aged five, and I well remember the happy days that Jane brought to us. The lively young girl brought some happiness back to our family, though my mother never fully recovered from Barbara's death. My father's answer to his grief was to plunge himself more and more into his work and his writing. Nonetheless, we owe much to Jane for the joy which she brought to us.

My father fought for a long time against the request that he should appear in religious television programmes. He perhaps had taken to heart the criticism one professor made of him in his student days: 'With a voice like *that* you'll never get anywhere!'

Dr Ronnie Falconer, Head of BBC Religious Television programmes, had experimented with a pilot programme and the group asked to evaluate it came out firmly against my father's style. But Dr Falconer was a man of vision and determination and he persevered. Eventually my father gave in and the famous William Barclay television series was the result.

In 1963 he started out on a series of TV programmes which entranced all those who watched them. The William Barclay Lectures on a Sunday evening became a national institution! He should have been a disaster with his heavy West of Scotland accent, his habit of continually walking up and down, and a host of other mannerisms which should have been off-putting for camera and audience alike!

The first pilot programmes had attempted to make him a talking head on screen, but Dr Falconer quickly realised that my father's appeal lay in his personality and lecturing style. It was a perfect example of success achieved by breaking all the rules and conventions!

It is interesting to note that my father's first radio broadcast goes back to 1949 and that he was successful in that medium too.

At 56 he became Professor of Divinity and Biblical Criticism at the University of Glasgow and there he remained until he retired in 1974. The manner of his appointment caused him the by now customary frustration and bewilderment that he was not recognised by his fellow academics. The unusually long time taken to make the appointment, caused probably by questions about his scholarship, left my father in no doubt at all that not everyone was in favour of him taking up this prestigious post.

Even at this moment of success, my father had to face much criticism. The scholars, as we have seen, felt that he was not expressing himself academically. The pillars of society felt that he was undermining the status quo. The radicals claimed he was not rejecting enough and the fundamentalists insisted that he was rejecting too much!

The fact that the millionth copy of the *Daily Study Bible* was printed in 1964 did not seem to matter to his critics and the controversy reached a climax when he turned down the nomination to be Moderator of the General Assembly of the Church of Scotland in 1967. He had no desire to hold high office or to become part of the Establishment and he could not bear the thought of being taken away from his students and his writing.

'It is not for me,' he said. His reaction to this nomination reveals the underlying naïveté in much that he did. He could not understand what all the fuss was about and his incurable optimism always made him act in a way which assumed other people would understand him and agree with his decisions. But this was not always the case.

My father was very much a family man, at home with the 'plain man' for whom he wrote. He was content to drive out to the seaside or to the moors, along with us and his beloved Rusty and sit there, reading, snoozing, perfectly at one with his family and his God. He did not like a fuss. The irony was, however, that no matter how hard he tried to avoid problems, they always cropped up throughout his life.

One honour in particular which thrilled him was the award of the Freedom of Motherwell and Wishaw in April 1967. I have many happy memories of Saturdays spent at the Motherwell football ground, Firpark, watching the boys in claret and amber either raise our souls heavenwards or plunge us into the depths of despair! To the end, my father loved his football and his home town. The citation to my father as an honorary burgess of the Burgh contains these words:

> *In recognition and appreciation of the distinguished services rendered by him in making the results of New Testament Scholarship known to a world-wide public through his teachings, writings, broadcasts and television appearances.*

The pace did not slacken as he grew older. His own New Testament translation appeared in 1967, the one book, he used to claim, that he did not write to order, but wrote because he *wanted* to write it!

But by 1969 his health was beginning to cause concern. All his life he had smoked too much and his lungs were giving warning signals. The doctors diagnosed emphysema. Far worse, their tests also revealed that he had Parkinson's Disease. The cruellest blow of all was their prognosis that he had eight years to live. I remember counting the years, the months, the weeks, the days. The doctors were right – he died eight years later, as they had forecast.

In 1969 my father was awarded the CBE, a great honour for Scotland's greatest communicator of the Bible and its truths.

The bad news about his health, however, was yet another moment where his happiness was blighted by misfortune and the suffering which had followed him since his childhood would not let him go. In a radio interview at this time he said that he believed in three things in life: work, our own faith, and that God helps us. When asked to describe his faith and beliefs further, he said: 'I believe in God, the world, that God cares, Jesus, the Holy Spirit, work, love, marriage, home, family, the Church.'

He was a man who constantly searched for new ways of exploring and expressing his beliefs.

My father retired from his Chair at the University of Glasgow on the 30th September 1974 and on the 1st October started work in the offices of William Collins, the publishers, in Glasgow, preparing a commentary on the Old Testament. Because of his failing health, only a few chapters on the Psalms were prepared. The book was published after his death under the title, *The Lord is my Shepherd*, the ultimate proof that, even in the days of illness and failing intellectual powers, my father was never far from his Maker and all that the Shepherd meant to him.

In April 1975 he received this citation from the Upper Room, Nashville, Tennessee:

Native son of Wick, Scotland.
Early master of New Testament studies
and teacher of preachers.
A prolific and disciplined writer with insight and power on the
*   meaning of prayer.*
Translator of the New Testament and expositor of relevant Biblical
*   applications.*
One who appreciates music
and trains and directs student choirs.
A lover of persons, whose focus is upon interpretations vividly and
*   strikingly stated.*
Effective and versatile communicator
*   of the Scriptures.*
Faithful disciple of Jesus Christ and untiring witness of His love
*   for all the world.*

There hardly could be a more fitting and appropriate tribute to a great communicator than the above.

The end came just after Christmas in 1977. I can remember those final days – his death came as a release from suffering. The once commanding, all-embracing presence had been reduced to a shell and the end came peacefully and gently on 24th January 1978.

He knew that it was coming, but he did not complain or protest. As he said goodbye to our elder daughter, who was returning to her au pair job in France shortly after the Christmas holidays, I could see that he knew it was the final farewell.

❖   ❖   ❖

As you read these pages, you will find reflections of a wonderful communicator, teacher, friend, husband, father and grandfather. You will find a man of immense talent and scholarship, and yet someone who was happiest when talking or writing about his beloved Jesus to the 'ordinary man and his wife'. His whole aim in life, he loved to sum up in Richard of Chichester's prayer:

> *To know Jesus Christ more clearly,*
> *To love him more dearly*
> *and to follow him more nearly.*

He was Christ's man. 'The others we know about,' he said. 'Jesus we know. The others we remember, Jesus we experience.'

One of the earliest memories of my childhood in the manse in Renfrew is of my father sitting at the piano singing his favourite hymns in a not-too tuneful voice and my mother telling him that he would annoy the neighbours, despite the fact that there was not a house near enough for anyone to hear! I can still hear him singing:

> *Lord of all being, throned afar,*
> *Thy glory flames from sun and star;*
> *Centre and soul of every sphere,*
> *Yet to each loving heart how near.*

It was my father's aim to bring that 'Lord of all being' to each 'loving heart' and he spent his life trying to achieve that aim.

Ronald Barclay
BEDFORD 1999

ADVENTURERS

WE should never be afraid of adventurous thought. If there is such a person as the Holy Spirit, God must ever be leading us into new truth. How would medicine fare if doctors were restricted to drugs and methods and techniques three hundred years old? And yet our standards of orthodoxy are far older than that. The man with something new has always to fight. Galileo, the seventeenth century astronomer and physicist, was branded a heretic when he held that the earth moved round the sun. Lister, the surgeon, had to fight for antiseptic technique in surgical operations. Simpson, also a surgeon, had to battle against opposition in the merciful use of chloroform. Let us have a care that when we resent new ideas we are not simply demonstrating that our minds are grown old and inelastic; and let us never shirk the adventure of thought.

We should never be afraid of new methods. That a thing has *always* been done may very well be the best reason for stopping doing it. That a thing has *never* been done may very well be the best reason for trying it. No business could exist on outworn methods – and yet the Church tries to. Any business which had lost as many customers as the Church has would have tried new ways long ago – but the Church tends to resent all that is new.

Once on a world tour Rudyard Kipling saw General Booth come aboard the ship. He came aboard to the beating of tambourines which Kipling's orthodox soul resented. Kipling got to know the General and told him how he disliked tambourines and all their kindred. Booth looked at him. 'Young man,' he said, 'if I thought I could win one more soul for Christ by standing on my head and beating a tambourine with my feet I would learn how to do it.'

There is a wise and an unwise conservatism. Let us have a care that in thought and in action we are not hidebound reactionaries when we ought, as Christians, to be gallant adventurers.

Luke 5: 36-39

AIMS

H G WELLS, the novelist, somewhere said, 'A man may be a bad musician and yet be passionately in love with music'. Robert Louis Stevenson spoke of even those who have sunk to the lowest depths 'clutching the remnants of virtue to them in the brothel and on the scaffold'. Sir Norman Birkett, the famous lawyer and judge, once, speaking of the criminals with whom he had come in contact in his work, spoke of the inextinguishable something in every man. Goodness, 'the implacable hunter', is always at their heels. The worst of men is 'condemned to some kind of nobility'.

The true wonder of man is not that he is a sinner, but that even in his sin he is haunted by goodness, that even in the mud he can never wholly forget the stars. David had always wished to build the Temple of God; he never achieved that ambition; it was denied and forbidden him; but God said to him, 'You did well that it was in your heart' (I Kings 8: 18). In his mercy God judges us, not only by our achievements, but also by our dreams. Even if a man never attains goodness, if to the end of the day he is still hungering and thirsting for it, he is not shut out from blessedness.

Matthew 5: 6

BLESSED are those who make this world a better place for all men to live in. Abraham Lincoln once said: 'Die when I may, I would like it to be said of me, that I always pulled up a weed and planted a flower where I thought a flower would grow.'

Matthew 5: 9

IN his autobiography H G Wells told of a crucial moment in his life. He was apprenticed to a draper, and there seemed to be little or no future for him. There came to him one day what he called an inward and prophetic voice: 'Get out of this trade before it is too late: at any cost get out of it.' He did not wait; he got out; and that is why he became H G Wells.

May God give to us that strength of decision which will save us from the tragedy of the unseized moment.

Matthew 8: 18-22

ANGER

JESUS condemns all selfish anger. The Bible is clear that anger is forbidden. 'The anger of man,' said James, 'does not work the righteousness of God' (James 1: 20). Paul orders his people to put off all 'anger, wrath, malice, slander' (Colossians 3: 8). Even the highest pagan thought saw the folly of anger. Cicero, the Roman orator and philosopher, said that when anger entered into the scene 'nothing could be done rightly and nothing sensibly'. In a vivid phrase the Roman philosopher Seneca called anger 'a brief insanity'.

So Jesus forbids for ever the anger which broods, the anger which will not forget, the anger which refuses to be pacified, the anger which seeks revenge. If we are to obey Jesus, all anger must be banished from life, and especially that anger which lingers too long. It is a warning thing to remember that no man can call himself a Christian and lose his temper because of any personal wrong which he has suffered. *Matthew 5: 21-22*

APPEARANCES

AGAIN and again men and women who became famous have been dismissed as non-entities. In his autobiography Gilbert Frankau tells how in the Victorian days his mother's house was a salon where the most brilliant people met. His mother arranged for the entertainment of her guests. Once she engaged a young Australian soprano to sing. After she had sung, Gilbert Frankau's mother said, 'What an appalling voice! She ought to be muzzled and allowed to sing no more!' The young singer's name was Nellie Melba.

Gilbert Frankau himself was producing a play. He sent to a theatrical agency for a young male actor to play the leading male part. The young man was interviewed and tested. After the test Frankau telephoned the agent. 'This man,' he said, 'will never do. He cannot act, and he never will be able to act, and you had better tell him to look for some other profession before he starves. By the way, tell me his name again so that I can cross him off my list.' The actor was Ronald Colman who was to become one of the most famous actors the screen has ever known.

Again and again people have been guilty of the most notorious moral misjudgments. Collie Knox tells of what happened to himself and a friend. He himself had been badly smashed up in a flying accident while serving in the Royal Flying Corps. The friend had that very day been decorated for gallantry at Buckingham Palace. They had changed from service dress into civilian clothes and were lunching together at a famous London restaurant, when a girl came up and handed to each of them a white feather – the badge of cowardice.

There is hardly anyone who has not been guilty of some grave misjudgment; there is hardly anyone who has not suffered from someone else's misjudgment. And yet the strange fact is that there is hardly any commandment of Jesus which is more consistently broken and neglected. *Matthew 7: 1-5*

AUTHORITY

IT is always wrong to regard people as things; it is always unchristian to regard people as cases. It was said of Beatrice Webb, afterwards Lady Passfield, the famous economist, that 'she saw men as specimens walking'. Dr Paul Tournier in *A Doctor's Casebook* talks of what he calls 'the personalism of the Bible'. He points out how fond the Bible is of names. God says to Moses: 'I know you by name' (Exodus 33: 17). God said to Cyrus: 'It is I, the God of Israel, who call you by your name'

(Isaiah 45: 3). There are whole pages of names in the Bible, Dr Tournier insists, that this is proof that the Bible thinks of people first and foremost, not as fractions of the mass, or abstractions or ideas, or cases, but as persons. 'The proper name,' Dr Tournier writes, 'is the symbol of the person. If I forget my patients' names, if I say to myself, "Ah! There's that gall-bladder type or that consumptive that I saw the other day", I am interesting myself more in their gall-bladders or in their lungs than in themselves as persons.' He insists that a patient must be always a person, and never a case.

God uses his authority to love men into goodness; to God no person ever becomes a thing. We must use such authority as we have always to understand and always at least to try to mend the person who has made the mistake; and we will never even begin to do that unless we remember that every man and woman is a person, not a thing.   *John 7: 53 - 8: 11*

AWARENESS OF GOD

BEFORE we can reverence God, we must not only believe that God is, we must also know the kind of God he is. No one could reverence the Greek gods with their loves and wars, their hates and adulteries, their trickeries and knaveries. No one can reverence capricious, immoral, impure gods. But in God as we know him there are three great qualities. There is *holiness;* there is *justice;* and there is *love.* We must reverence God, not only because he exists, but because he is the God whom we know him to be.

But a man might believe that God is; he might be intellectually convinced that God is holy, just and loving; and still he might not have reverence. For reverence there is necessary *a constant awareness of God.* To reverence God means to live in a God-filled world, to live a life in which we never forget God. This awareness is not confined to the Church or to so-called holy places: it must be an awareness which exists everywhere and at all times.

The poet William Wordsworth spoke of it in 'Lines composed near Tintern Abbey':

... And I have felt
A presence that disturbs me with the joy
Of elevated thoughts: a sense sublime
Of something far more deeply interfused.
Whose dwelling is the light of setting suns.
And the round ocean, and the living air.
And the blue sky, and in the mind of man:
A motion and a spirit, that impels
All thinking things, all objects of all thought.
And rolls through all things.

One of the finest of modern devotional poets is Henry Ernest Hardy, who wrote under the name of Father Andrew. In 'The Mystic Beauty' he writes:

O London town has many moods,
And mingled 'mongst its many broods
A leavening of saints,

And ever up and down its streets,
If one has eyes to see one meets
Stuff that an artist paints.
I've seen a back street bathed in blue,
Such as the soul of Whistler knew:
A smudge of amber light,

Where some fried fish-shop plied its trade,
A perfect note of colour made –
Oh, it was exquisite!

I once came through St James's Park
Betwixt the sunset and the dark
And oh the mystery

Of grey and green and violet!
I would I never might forget
That evening harmony.

I hold it true that God is there
If beauty breaks through anywhere;
And his most blessed feet.

Who once life's roughest roadway trod,
Who came as man to show us God,
Still pass along the street.

God in the back street, God in St James's Park, God in the fried fish-shop – that is reverence. The trouble with most people is that their awareness of God is spasmodic, acute at certain times and places, totally absent at others. Reverence means the constant awareness of God.

Matthew 6: 9

BEGINNING

FOR us the great value of a child must always lie in the possibilities locked up within him. Everything depends on how he is taught and trained. The possibilities may never be realised; they may be stifled and stunted; that which might be used for good may be deflected to the purposes of evil; or they may be unleashed in such a way that a new tide of power floods the earth.

Away back in the eleventh century, Duke Robert of Burgundy was one of the great warrior and knightly figures. He was about to go off on a campaign. He had a baby son who was his heir; and, before he departed, he made his barons and nobles come and swear fealty to the little infant, in the event of anything happening to himself. They came with their waving plumes and their clanking armour and knelt before the child. One great baron smiled and Duke Robert asked him why. He said, 'The child is so little'. 'Yes,' said Duke Robert, 'he's little – but he'll grow.' Indeed he grew, for that baby became William the Conqueror of England.

In every child there are infinite possibilities for good or ill. It is the supreme responsibility of the parent, of the teacher, of the Christian Church, to see that his dynamic possibilities for good are realised. To stifle them, to leave them untapped, to twist them into evil powers, is sin.   *Matthew 18: 8-9*

BEAUTY OF THE WORLD

ONE of the finest things ever said is the Rabbinic saying, 'A man will have to give an account on the judgment day for every good thing which he might have enjoyed, and did not'.

Dr Boreham has a story which is a commentary on the wrong idea of fasting. A traveller in the Rocky mountains fell in with an old Roman Catholic priest; he was amazed to find so aged a man struggling amidst the rocks and the precipices and the steep passes. The traveller asked the priest, 'What are you doing here?'

The old man answered, 'I am seeking the beauty of the world'.

'But,' said the traveller, surely you have left it very late in life?'

So the old man told his story. He had spent nearly all his life in a monastery; he had never been further outside it than the cloisters. He fell seriously ill, and in his illness he had a vision. He saw an angel stand beside his bed. 'What have you come for?' he asked the angel.

'To lead you home,' the angel said.

'And is it a very beautiful world to which I am going?' asked the old man.

'It is a very beautiful world you are leaving,' said the angel.

'And then,' said the old man, 'I remembered that I had seen nothing of it except the fields and the trees around the monastery.' So he said to the angel, 'But I have seen very little of the world which I am leaving'.

'Then,' said the angel, 'I fear you will see very little beauty in the world to which you are going.'

'I was in trouble,' said the old man, 'and I begged that I might stay for just two more years. My prayer was granted, and I am spending all my little hoard of gold, and all the time I have, in exploring the world's loveliness – and I find it very wonderful!'

It is the duty of a man to accept and enjoy the world's love-liness, and not to reject it. *Matthew 6: 16-18*

BORN AGAIN

CONSIDER the effect of Jesus on a man. The very first effect is to make him see his own utter unworthiness in comparison with the beauty and the loveliness of the life of Jesus. 'Depart from me,' said Peter, 'for I am a sinful man' (Luke 5: 8). When Tockichi Ishii first read the story of the Gospel, he said 'I stopped. I was stabbed to the heart as if pierced by a five-inch nail. Shall I call it the love of Christ? Shall I call it his compassion? I do not know what to call it. I only know that I believed and my hard-ness of heart was changed.' The first reaction was that he was stabbed to the heart. The result of that sense of unworthiness and the result of that stabbed heart is a heart-felt penitence, and peni-tence is the only condition of forgiveness. But, if a man has got himself into such a state, by repeated refusals to listen to the promptings of the Holy Spirit, that he cannot see anything lovely in Jesus at all, then the sight of Jesus will not give him any sense of sin; because he has no sense of sin he cannot be penitent, and because he is not penitent he cannot be forgiven.

One of the Lucifer legends tells how one day a priest noticed in his congregation a magnificently handsome young man. After the service the young man stayed for confession. He confessed so many and such terrible sins that the priest's hair stood on end.

'You must have lived long to have done all that,' the priest said.

'My name is Lucifer and I fell from heaven at the beginning of time,' said the young man.

'Even so,' said the priest, 'say that you are sorry, say that you repent and even you can be forgiven.' The young man looked at the priest for a moment and then turned and strode away. He would not and could not say it; and therefore he had to go on still desolate and still damned.

There is only one condition of forgiveness and that is penitence. So long as a man sees loveliness in Christ, so long as he hates his sin even if he cannot leave it, even if he is in the mud and the mire, he can still be forgiven. But if a man, by repeated refusals of God's guidance, has lost the ability to recognise goodness when he sees it; if he has got his moral values inverted until evil to him is good and good to him is evil, then, even when he is confronted by Jesus, he is conscious of no sin; he cannot repent and therefore he can never be forgiven. That is the sin against the Holy Spirit.

Mark 3: 28-30

CALL OF GOD

IT can happen that a man loves his wife and his family so much that he may refuse some great adventure, some avenue of service, some call to sacrifice, either because he does not wish to leave them, or because to accept it would involve them in danger. T R Glover quotes a letter from Oliver Cromwell to Lord Wharton. The date is 1st January 1649, and Cromwell had in the back of his mind that Wharton might be so attached to his home and to his wife that he might refuse to hear the call to adventure and to battle, and might choose to stay at home: 'My service to the dear little lady; I wish you make her not a greater temptation than she is. Take heed of all relations. Mercies should not be temptations; yet we too often make them so.'

It has happened that a man has refused God's call to some adventurous bit of service, because he allowed personal attachments to immobilise him. Lovelace, the cavalier poet, writes to his Lucasta, 'Going to the Wars':

> Tell me not (Sweet) I am unkind,
>   That from the nunnery
> Of thy chaste breast, and quiet mind,
>   To war and arms I fly.
>
> True; a new mistress now I chase,
>   The first foe in the field;
> And with a stronger faith embrace
>   A sword, a horse, a shield.
> Yet this inconstancy is such,
>   As you too shall adore.
> I could not love thee (Dear) so much,
>   Loved I not honour more.

It is very seldom any man is confronted with this choice; he may well go through life and never face it; but the fact remains that it is possible for a man's loved ones to become in effect his enemies, if the thought of them keeps him from doing what he knows God wants him to do.

He offers a *choice;* and a man has to choose sometimes between the closest ties of earth and loyalty to Jesus Christ.

Bunyan knew all about that choice. The thing which troubled him most about his imprisonment was the effect it would have upon his wife and children. What was to happen to them, bereft of his support. 'The parting with my wife and poor children hath often been to me in this place, as the pulling the flesh from my bones; and that not only because I am somewhat too fond of these great mercies, but also because I should have often brought to my mind the many hardships, miseries, and wants that my poor family was like to meet with, should I be taken from them, *especially my poor blind child*, who lay nearer my heart than all I had besides. O the thought of the hardship I thought my blind one might go under, would break up my heart to pieces .... But yet, recalling myself, thought I, I must venture you all with God, though it goeth to the quick to leave you; O I saw in this condition, I was a man who was pulling down his house upon the head of his wife and children; yet thought I, I must do it, I must do it.'

Once again, this terrible choice will come very seldom; in God's mercy to many of us it may never come; but the fact remains that all loyalties must give place to loyalty to God.

Matthew 10: 34-39

CHANCES MISSED

IN every life there come moments of decision which may be accepted or rejected. To accept them is to succeed; to reject, or to shirk them, is to fail. Lowell, the American poet, wrote:

Once to every man and nation comes the moment to decide.
In the strife of Truth with falsehood, for the good or evil side.
Some great cause, God's new Messiah, offering each the bloom or blight,
Parts the goats upon the left hand, and the sheep upon the right
And the choice goes by for ever 'twixt that darkness and that light.

To every man there comes the unreturning decisive moment. As Shakespeare saw it:

> *There is a tide in the affairs of men*
> *Which, taken at the flood, leads on to fortune;*
> *Omitted, all the voyage of their lives*
> *Is bound in shallows and in miseries.*

The undecided life is the wasted life, the frustrated life, the discontented life, and often the tragic life. John Oxenham wrote:

> *To every man there openeth*
> *A way and ways and a way;*
> *The high soul treads the high way,*
> *And the low soul gropes the low,*
> *And in between on the misty flats,*
> *The rest drift to and fro.*

The drifting life can never be the happy life. Jesus knew when John emerged that the moment of decision had come. Nazareth was peaceful and home was sweet, but he answered the summons and the challenge of God.

It was the moment of *identification*. It is true that Jesus did not need to repent from sin; but here was a movement of the people back to God; and with that Godward movement he was determined to identify himself. A man might himself possess ease and comfort and wealth and still identify himself with a movement to bring better things to the downtrodden and the poor and the ill-housed and the over-worked and the underpaid. The really great identification is when a man identifies himself with a movement, not for his own sake, but for the sake of others. In John Bunyan's dream, Christian came in his journeying with Interpreter to the Palace which was heavily guarded and required a battle to seek an entry. At the door there sat the man with the inkhorn taking the names of those who would dare the assault. All were hanging back. Then Christian saw 'a man of a very stout countenance come up to the man that sat there to write, saying, "Set down my name, sir"'.' When great things are afoot the Christian is bound to say, 'Set down my name, sir', for that is what Jesus did when he came to be baptised. *Mark 1: 9-11*

CHRIST

MURETUS was a wandering scholar of the middle ages. He was poor. In an Italian town he took ill and was taken to a hospital for waifs and strays. The doctors were discussing his case in Latin, never dreaming he could understand. They suggested that since he was such a worthless wanderer they might use him for medical experiments. He looked up and answered them in their own learned tongue, 'Call no man worthless for whom Christ died.' *Luke 1: 57-66*

IT is not only at the communion table we can be with Christ; we can be with him at the dinner table too. He is not only the host in his Church; he is the guest in every home. Fay Inchfawn wrote:

Sometimes, when everything goes wrong;
When days are short and nights are long;
When wash day brings so dull a sky
That not a single thing will dry.
And when the kitchen chimney smokes,
And when there's naught so 'queer' as folks!
When friends deplore my faded youth,
And when the baby cuts a tooth.
While John, the baby last but one,
Clings round my skirts till day is done;
And fat, good-tempered Jane is glum,
And butcher's man forgets to come.
Sometimes I say on days like these,
I get a sudden gleam of bliss.

Not on some sunny day of ease,
He'll come ... but on a day like this!

The Christian lives always and everywhere in a Christ-filled world.

Luke 24: 13

❖   ❖   ❖

TO accept the offer of Jesus Christ is to find life. Everyone in one sense may be said to be alive; but there are few who can be said to know life in the real sense of the term. When Grenfell was writing to a nursing sister about her decision to come out to Labrador to help in his work there, he told her that he could not offer her much money, but that if she came she would discover that if serving Christ and the people of the country she would have the time of her life.

Browning describes the meeting of two people into whose hearts love had entered. She looked at him, he looked at her, and 'suddenly life awoke'. A modern novelist makes one character say to another: 'I never knew what life was till I saw it in your eyes.'

The person who accepts the way of Christ has passed from death to life. In this world life becomes new and thrilling; in the world to come eternal life with God becomes a certainty.

John 5: 24

CHRISTIANITY

THERE are four great social directions in which Christianity transformed life. Christianity transformed life for *women*. The Jew in his morning prayer thanked God that he had not made him a Gentile, a slave or a woman. In Greek civilisation the woman lived a life of utter seclusion, with nothing to do beyond the household tasks. K J Freeman writes of the life of the Greek child or young man even in the great days of Athens: 'When he came home, there was no home life. His father was hardly ever in the house. His mother was a nonentity, living in the women's apartments; he probably saw little of her.' In the eastern lands it was often possible to see a family on a journey. The father would be mounted on an ass; the mother would be walking, and probably bent beneath a burden. One demonstrable historical truth is that Christianity transformed life for women.

Christianity transformed life for *the weak and the ill*. In heathen life the weak and the ill were considered a nuisance. In Sparta a child, when he was born, was submitted to the examiners: if he was fit, he was allowed to live; if he was weakly or deformed, he was exposed to death on the mountain side. Dr A Rendle Short points out that the first blind asylum was founded by Thalasius, a Christian monk; the first free dispensary was founded by Apollonius, a Christian merchant; the first hospital of which there is any record was founded by Fabiola, a Christian lady. Christianity was the first faith to be interested in the broken things of life.

Christianity transformed life for *the aged*. Like the weak, the aged were a nuisance. Cato, the Roman writer on agriculture, gives advice to anyone who is taking over a farm: 'Look over the livestock and hold a sale. Sell your oil if the price is satisfactory, and sell the surplus of your wine and grain. Sell worn-out oxen, blemished cattle, blemished sheep, wool hides, an old wagon, old tools, *an old slave, a sickly slave*, and whatever else is superfluous.'

The old, whose day's work was done, were fit for nothing else than to be discarded on the rubbish heaps of life. Christianity was the first faith to regard men as persons and not instruments capable of doing so much work.

Christianity transformed life for *the child*. In the immediate background of Christianity, the marriage relationship had broken down, and the home was in peril. Divorce was so common that it was neither unusual nor particularly blameworthy for a woman to have a new husband every year. In such circumstances children were a disaster; and the custom of simply exposing children to death was tragically common. There is a well-known letter from a man Hilarion, who had gone off to Alexandria, to his wife Alis, whom he has left at home. He writes to her: 'If – good luck to you – you bear a child, if it is a boy, let it live; if it is a girl, throw it out.' In modern civilisation, life is almost built round the child; in ancient civilisation the child had a very good chance of dying before it had begun to live.

Anyone who asks the question – 'What has Christianity done for the world?' – has delivered himself into a Christian debater's hands. There is nothing in history so unanswerably demonstrable as the transforming power of Christianity and of Christ on the individual life and on the life of society.   *Matthew 13: 33*

THE greatest and the most obvious quality of salt is that *salt lends flavour to things.* Food without salt is a sadly insipid, even a sickening thing. Christianity is to life what salt is to food. Christianity lends flavour to life.

The tragedy is that so often people have connected Christianity with precisely the opposite. They have connected Christianity with that which takes the flavour out of life. Swinburne, the English poet, had it:

> *Thou hast conquered, O pale Galilaean*
> *The world has grown gray from Thy breath.*

Even after Constantine had made Christianity the religion of the Roman Empire, there came to the throne another Emperor called Julian, who wished to put the clock back and to bring back the old gods. His complaint, as the Norwegian dramatist Ibsen puts it, was:

> *Have you looked at these Christians closely? Hollow-eyed, pale-cheeked, flat-breasted all; they brood their lives away, unspurred by ambition; the sun shines for them, but they do not see it; the earth offers them its fulness, but they desire it not; all their desire is to renounce and to suffer that they may come to die.*

As Julian saw it, Christianity took the vividness out of life.

Oliver Wendell Holmes once said, 'I might have entered the ministry if certain clergymen I knew had not looked and acted so much like undertakers'. Robert Louis Stevenson once entered in his diary, as if he was recording an extraordinary phenomenon, 'I have been to Church today, and am not depressed'.

Men need to discover the lost radiance of the Christian faith. In a worried world, the Christian should be the only man who remains serene. In a depressed world, the Christian should be the only man who remains full of the joy of life. There should be a sheer sparkle about the Christian, but too often he dresses like a mourner at a funeral, and talks like a spectre at a feast. Wherever he is, if he is to be the salt of the earth, the Christian must be the diffuser of joy. *Matthew 5: 13*

COMMITMENT

IT is fatally easy to become set in our ways. A man called I A Findlay quotes a saying of one of his friends – 'When you reach a conclusion you're dead.' What he meant was that when our minds become fixed and settled in their ways, when they are quite unable to accept new truth and to contemplate new ways, we may be physically alive but we are mentally dead.

As they grow older, almost everyone develops a constitutional dislike of that which is new and unfamiliar. We grow very unwilling to make any adjustments in our habits and ways of life. Lesslie Newbigin, who was involved in the discussions about the formation of the United Church of South India, tells how one of the things that most often held things up was that people kept asking, 'Now, if we do that, just where are we going?'

In the end someone had to say bluntly, 'The Christian has no right to ask where he is going'. Abraham went out not knowing whither he went (Hebrews 11: 8). There is a great verse in that same chapter of Hebrews: 'By faith Jacob, when dying, blessed each of the sons of Joseph bowing in worship over the head of his staff' (Hebrews 11: 21). With the very breath of death upon him, the old traveller still had his pilgrim staff in his hand. To the end of the day, with the evening now upon him, he was still ready for the road.

If we are really to rise to the height of the Christian challenge, we must retain the adventurous mind. I received a letter once which ended 'yours aged 83 and still growing' – and with the inexhaustible riches of Christ before us, why not?

Mark 2: 21-22

JESUS knew what was going to happen. That is his supreme courage, especially in the last days. It would have been easy for him to escape, and yet, undeterred, he went on. The classical poet Homer relates how the great warrior Achilles was told that if he went out to his last battle, he would surely be killed. His answer was: 'Nevertheless I am for going on.' With a full knowledge of what lay ahead, Jesus was for going on.   *Mark 14: 17-21*

IT is a tremendous thing about Jesus that there was nothing for which he was not prepared. The opposition, the misunderstanding, the enmity of the orthodox religious people, the betrayal by one of his own inner circle, the pain and the agony of the Cross – he was prepared for them all. But perhaps what hurt him most was the failure of his friends. It is when a man is up against it that he needs his friends most, and that was exactly when Jesus' friends left him all alone and let him down. There was nothing in the whole gamut of physical pain and mental torture that Jesus did not pass through.

Sir Hugh Walpole wrote a great novel called *Fortitude*, the story of one called Peter, whose creed was, 'It isn't life that matters, but the courage you bring to it'. Life did everything that it possibly could to him. At the end, on his own mountain top, he heard a voice, 'Blessed be pain and torment and every torture of the body. Blessed be all loss and the failure of friends and the sacrifice of love. Blessed be all failure and the ruin of every earthly hope. Blessed be all sorrow and torment, hardships, and endurances that demand courage. Blessed be these things – for of these things cometh the making of a man.'

Peter fell to praying: 'Make of me a man ... to be afraid of nothing, to be ready for everything. Love, friendship, success ... to take it if it comes, to care nothing if these things are not for me. Make me brave. Make me brave.'

Jesus had supremely, more than anyone who ever lived, this quality of fortitude, this ability to remain erect no matter with what blows life assaulted him, this serenity when there was nothing but heartbreak behind and torture in front. Inevitably, every now and then, we find ourselves catching our breath at his sheer heroism.

When Jesus foretold this tragic failure of loyalty, Peter could not believe that it would happen. In the days of the Stewart troubles they captured the Cock of the North, the Marquis of Huntly. They pointed at the block and the axe and told him that unless he abandoned his loyalty he would be executed then and there. His answer was, 'You can take my head from my shoulders, but you will never take my heart from my king'. That is what Peter said that night.   *Mark 14: 27-31*

THE CROSS

THE great truth is that, wherever Jesus Christ is, the wildest storm becomes a calm. Olive Wyon, in her book *Consider Him,* quotes a thing from the letters of St Francis of Sales. St Francis had noticed a custom of the country district in which he lived. He had often noticed a farm servant going across a farmyard to draw water at the well; he also noticed that, before she lifted the brimming pail, the girl always put a piece of wood into it. One day he went out to the girl and asked her, 'Why do you do that?' She looked surprised and answered, as if it were a matter of course, 'Why? To keep the water from spilling ... to keep it steady!' Writing to a friend later on, the bishop told this story and added: 'So when your heart is distressed and agitated, put the Cross into its centre to keep it steady!'

In every time of storm and stress, the presence of Jesus, and the love which flows from the Cross, bring peace and serenity and calm.   *Matthew 14: 28-33*

❖   ❖   ❖

LEGEND calls the penitent thief Dismas, and tells that he did not meet Jesus for the first time when they both hung on their crosses on Calvary. The story runs like this –

When Joseph and Mary were on their way to Egypt, they were waylaid by robbers. One of the robber chiefs wished to murder them at once and to steal their little store of goods. But something about the baby Jesus went straight to Dismas' heart, for Dismas was one of these robbers. He refused to allow any harm to come to Jesus or his parents. He looked at Jesus and said, 'O most blessed of children, if ever there comes a time for having mercy on me, then remember me, and forget not this hour'.

So, the legend says, Jesus and Dismas met again at Calvary, and Dismas on the cross found forgiveness and mercy for his soul.   *Matthew 2: 13-15*

❖   ❖   ❖

SO there was on Golgotha a group of three crosses: in the middle the Son of God, and on either side a brigand. Truly, he was with sinners in his death.

The final verses describe the taunts flung at Jesus by the passers-by, by the Jewish authorities, and by the brigands who were crucified with him. They all centred round one thing – the claims that Jesus had made and his apparent helplessness on the Cross. It was precisely there that the Jews were so wrong. They were using the glory of Christ as a means of mocking him. 'Come down,' they said, 'and we will believe in you.' But as General Booth once said, 'It is precisely because he would not come down that we believe in him'. The Jews could see God only in power; but Jesus showed that God is sacrificial love.

Matthew 27: 32-44

DECISIONS

FOR Jesus it was true that he had to press on with God's work in the day, for the night of the Cross lay close ahead. But it is true for every man. We are given only so much time. Whatever we are to do must be done within it.

There is in Glasgow a sundial with the motto: 'Tak' tent of time ere time be tint' – 'Take thought of time before time is ended.' We should never put things off until another time, for another time may never come. The Christian's duty is to fill the time he has – and no man knows how much that will be – with the service of God and of his fellow men. There is no more poignant sorrow than the tragic discovery that it is too late to do something which we might have done.

But there is another opportunity we may miss. Jesus said: 'So long as I am in the world, I am the light of the world.' When Jesus said that, he did not mean that the time of his life and work were limited, but that our opportunity of laying hold on him is limited. There comes to every man a chance to accept Christ as his Saviour, his Master, and his Lord; and if that opportunity is not seized, it may well never come back.

E D Starbuck in *The Psychology of Religion* has some interesting and warning statistics about the age at which conversion normally occurs. It can occur as early as seven or eight; it increases gradually to the age of ten or eleven; it increases rapidly to the age of sixteen; it declines steeply up to the age of twenty; and after thirty it is very rare. God is always saying to us: *'Now* is the time.' It is not that the power of Jesus grows less, or that his light grows dim; it is that if we put off the great decision, we become ever less able to take it as the years go on. Work must be done, decisions must be taken, while it is day, before the night comes down.

John 9: 1-5

DETERIORATION

THERE is a terrible story about an artist who was painting the Last Supper. It was a great picture and it took him many years. As a model for the face of Christ, he used a young man with a face of transcendent loveliness and purity. Bit by bit the picture was filled in, and one after another the disciples were painted.

The day came when he needed a model for Judas whose face he had left to the last. He went out and searched in the lowest haunts of the city and in the dens of vice. At last he found a man with a face so depraved and vicious as matched his requirement.

When the sittings were at an end, the man said to the artist: 'You painted me before.' 'Surely not,' said the artist. 'O yes,' said the man, 'I sat for your Christ.' The years had brought terrible deterioration.

John 6: 66-71

THE DEVIL

HERE, then, is one of the great and precious truths about temptation. Temptation is not designed to make us fall. Temptation is designed to make us stronger and better men and women. Temptation is not designed to make us sinners. It is designed to make us good. We may fail in the test, but we are not meant to. We are meant to emerge stronger and finer. In one sense temptation is not so much the *penalty* of being a man: it is the *glory* of being a man. If metal is to be used in a great engineering project, it is tested at stresses and strains far beyond those which it is ever likely to have to bear. So a man has to be tested before God can use him greatly in his service.

All that is true; but it is also true that the Bible is never in any doubt that there is a power of evil in this world. The Bible is not a speculative book, and it does not discuss the origin of that power of evil, but it knows that it is there. Quite certainly the petition of the Lord's Prayer should be translated not 'Deliver us from evil', but 'Deliver us from the Evil One'. The Bible does not think of evil as an abstract principle or force, but as an active, personal power in opposition to God.

The development of the idea of Satan in the Bible is of the greatest interest. In Hebrew the word *Satan* simply means an *adversary*. It can often be used of men. A man's adversary is his *Satan*. In the Authorised Version, the Philistines are afraid that David may turn out to be their *Satan* (1 Samuel 29: 4); Solomon declares that God has given him such peace and prosperity that there is no *Satan* left to oppose him (1 Kings 5: 4); David regards Abishai as his *Satan* (2 Samuel 19: 22). In all these cases *Satan* means an *adversary* or *opponent*.

From that, the word *Satan* goes on to mean *one who pleads a case against someone*. Then the word leaves earth and, as it were, enters heaven. The Jews had the idea that in heaven there was an angel whose charge it was to state the case against a man, a kind of prosecuting angel; and that became the function of *Satan*. At that stage Satan is not an evil power; he is part of the judgment apparatus of heaven. In Job 1: 6, Satan is numbered among the sons of God: 'Now there was a day when the sons of God came to present themselves before the Lord, and Satan also came among them.' At this stage Satan is the divine prosecutor of man.

But it is not so very far a step from *stating* a case against a man to *making up a case* against a man. And that is the next step. The other name of Satan is *the Devil*; and *Devil* comes from the Greek word *Diabolos,* which is the regular word for *a slanderer.* So *Satan* becomes the *Devil,* the *slanderer par excellence,* the adversary of man, the power who is out to frustrate the purposes of God and to ruin mankind. Satan comes to stand for everything which is anti-man and anti-God.

It is from that ruining power that Jesus teaches us to pray to be delivered. The origin of that power is not discussed; there are no speculations. As someone has put it: 'If a man wakes up and finds his house on fire, he does not sit down in a chair and write or read a treatise on the origin of fires in private houses; he sets out to try to extinguish the fire and to save his house.' So the Bible wastes no time in speculations about the origin of evil.

It equips man to fight the battle against the evil which is unquestionably there.

Matthew 6: 13

DOMESTICATE GOD

GREEN Armytage, in his book *A Portrait of St Luke,* speaks of how Luke delighted to show Jesus against a background of simple, homely things and people. In a vivid phrase, he says that St Luke's gospel 'domesticated God'; it brought God right into the home circle and into the ordinary things of life. Jesus's action at Cana of Galilee shows what he thought of a home. As the Revised Standard Version has it, he 'manifested forth his glory', and that manifestation took place within a home.

There is a strange paradox in the attitude of many people to the place they call home. They would admit at once that there is no more precious place in all the world; and yet, at the same time, they would also have to admit that in it they claim the right to be far more discourteous, far more boorish, far more selfish, far more impolite than they would dare to be in any society of strangers. Many of us treat the ones we love most in a way that we would never dare to treat a chance acquaintance. So often it is strangers who see us at our best, and those who live with us who see us at our worst.

We ought ever to remember that it was in a humble home that Jesus manifested forth his glory. To him home was a place for which nothing but his best was good enough.

John 2: 1-11

DO UNTO OTHERS

IT is perfectly possible for a man of the world to observe the negative form of the golden rule. He could, without very serious difficulty, so discipline his life that he would not do to others what he did not wish them to do to him; but the only man who can even begin to satisfy the positive form of the rule is the man who has the love of Christ within his heart. He will try to forgive as he would wish to be forgiven, to help as he would wish to be helped, to praise as he would wish to be praised, to understand as he would wish to be understood. He will never seek to avoid doing things: he will always look for things to do.

Clearly this will make life much more complicated; clearly he will have much less time to spend on his own desires and his own activities – for time and time again he will have to stop what he is doing to help someone else. It will be a principle which will dominate his life at home, in the factory, in the bus, in the office, in the street, in the train, at his games, everywhere. He can never do it until self withers and dies within his heart. To obey this commandment a man must become a new man with a new centre to his life; and if the world was composed of people who sought to obey this rule, it would be a new world.

Matthew 7: 12

DUTY

LET the tax-collector be a good tax-collector; let the soldier be a good soldier. It was a man's duty to serve God where God had set him. A negro spiritual says:

> *There's a king and captain high,*
> *And he's coming by and by,*
> *And he'll find me hoeing cotton when he comes,*
> *You can hear his legions charging in the regions of the sky,*
> *And he'll find me hoeing cotton when he comes.*
> *There's a man they thrust aside,*
> *Who was tortured till he died,*
> *And he'll find me hoeing cotton when he comes.*
> *He was hated and rejected,*
> *He was scorned and crucified,*
> *And he'll find me hoeing cotton when he comes.*

When he comes! when he comes!
He'll be crowned by saints and angels when he comes.
They'll be shouting out Hosanna! to the man that men denied,
And I'll kneel among my cotton when he comes.

It was John's conviction that nowhere can a man serve God better than in his day's work.

Luke 3: 7-18

JESUS came into the world to be the Saviour of the world, and for thirty years he never moved beyond the bounds of Palestine, except to the Passover at Jerusalem. He died when he was thirty-three, and of these thirty-three years thirty were spent without record in Nazareth. To put it in another way, ten-elevenths of Jesus' life were spent in Nazareth. What was happening then?

Jesus was growing up to boyhood, and then to manhood, in a good home; and there can be no greater start to life than that. J S Blackie, the famous Edinburgh professor, once said in public, 'I desire to thank God for the good stock-in-trade, so to speak, which I inherited from my parents for the business of life'. George Herbert once said, 'A good mother is worth a hundred schoolmasters'. So for Jesus the years passed, silently but mouldingly, in the circle of a good home.

Jesus was fulfilling the duties of an eldest son. It seems most likely that Joseph died before the family had grown up. Maybe he was already much older than Mary when they married. In the story of the Wedding Feast at Cana of Galilee, there is no mention of Joseph, although Mary is there, and it is natural to suppose that Joseph had died.

So Jesus became the village craftsman of Nazareth to support his mother and his younger brothers and sisters. A world was calling him, and yet he first fulfilled his duty to his mother and to his own folks and to his own home. When his mother died, Sir James Barrie, the author of *Peter Pan*, could write, 'I can look back, and I cannot see the smallest thing undone'. There lies happiness. It is on those who faithfully and ungrudgingly accept the simple duties that the world is built.

One of the great examples of that is the great doctor, Sir James Young Simpson, the discoverer of chloroform. He came from a poor home. One day his mother took him on her knee and began to darn his stockings. When she had finished, she looked at her neat handiwork. 'My, Jamie,' she said, 'mind when your mither's awa' that she was a grand darner.' Jamie was the 'wise wean, the little box of brains', and his family knew it. They had their dreams for him. His brother Sandy said, 'I aye felt he would be great some day'. And so, without jealousy and willingly, his brothers worked in the bakeshop and at their jobs that the lad might have his college education and his chance. There would have been no Sir James Simpson had there not been simple folk willing to do simple things and to deny themselves so that the brilliant lad might have his chance.

Jesus is the great example of one who accepted the simple duties of the home.   *Matthew 2: 23 to 3: 1*

DIGNITY

THERE is a famous story of Diogenes, the Cynic philosopher. He was captured by pirates and was being sold as a slave. As he gazed at the bystanders who were bidding for him, he looked at a man. 'Sell me to that man,' he said. 'He needs a master.' The man bought him; handed over the management of his household and the education of his children to him. 'It was a good day for me,' he used to say, 'when Diogenes entered my household.' True, but that required an abrogation of dignity.

It frequently happens that a man stands on his dignity and falls from grace.   *Mark 5: 21-24*

DISCIPLINE

NOTHING was ever achieved without discipline, and many an athlete and many a man has been ruined because he abandoned discipline and let himself grow slack. Samuel Taylor Coleridge, the English Romantic poet, is the supreme tragedy of indiscipline. Never did so great a mind produce so little. He left Cambridge University to join the army, he left the army because, in spite of all his erudition, he could not rub down a horse; he returned to Oxford and left without a degree. He began a paper called *The Watchman* which lived for ten numbers and then died. It has been said of him: 'He lost himself in visions of work to be done, that always remained to be done. Coleridge had every poetic gift, but one – the gift of sustained and concentrated effort.' In his head and in his mind he had all kinds of books, as he said himself, 'completed save for transcription' …. 'I am on the eve,' he says, 'of sending to the press two octavo volumes.' But the books were never composed outside Coleridge's mind, because he would not face the discipline of sitting down to write them out.

No one ever reached any eminence, and no one having reached it ever maintained it, without discipline.

Matthew 7: 13-14

EXAMPLE

WHEN a man sows the seed of the word, he does not know what he is doing or what effect the seed is having. H L Gee tells this story. In the church where he worshipped, there was a lonely old man, old Thomas. He had outlived all his friends and hardly anyone knew him. When Thomas died, Gee had the feeling that there would be no one to go to the funeral, so he decided to go, so that there might be someone to follow the old man to his last resting-place.

There was no one else and it was a wild, wet day. The funeral reached the cemetery; and at the gate there was a soldier waiting. He was an officer, but on his raincoat there were no rank badges. The soldier came to the graveside for the ceremony; when it was over he stepped forward and before the open grave swept his hand to a salute that might have been given to a king. H L Gee walked away with this soldier, and as they walked the wind blew the soldier's raincoat open to reveal the shoulder badges of a brigadier.

The brigadier said to Gee: 'You will perhaps be wondering what I am doing here. Years ago, Thomas was my Sunday School teacher; I was a wild lad and a sore trial to him. He never knew what he did for me, but I owe everything I am or will be to old Thomas, and today I had to come to salute him at the end.'

Thomas did not know what he was doing. No preacher or teacher ever does. It is our task to sow the seed and leave the rest to God. *Matthew 13: 1-9 to 18: 23*

CECIL Northcott, in *Famous Life Decisions,* tells of what Kagawa, the Japanese writer, did. He went to live in a six-foot-by-six hut in a Tokyo slum. 'On his first night he was asked to share his bed with a man suffering from a contagious itch. That was a test of his faith. Would he go back on his point of no return? No. He welcomed his bed-fellow. Then a beggar asked for his shirt, and got it. Next day he was back for Kagawa's coat and trousers, and got them too. Kagawa was left standing in a ragged old kimono. The slum dwellers of Tokyo laughed at him, but they came to respect him. He stood in the driving rain to preach, coughing all the time. "God is love," he shouted. "God is love. Where love is, there is God." He often fell down exhausted, and the rough men of the slums carried him gently back to his hut.'

Kagawa himself wrote: 'God dwells among the lowliest of men. He sits on the dust heap among the prison convicts. He stands with the juvenile delinquents. He is there with the beggars. He is among the sick, he stands with the unemployed. Therefore let him who would meet God visit the prison cell before going to the temple. Before he goes to Church let him visit the hospital. Before he reads his Bible let him help the beggar.'

Therein is greatness. The world may assess a man's greatness by the number of people whom he controls and who are at his beck and call; or by his intellectual standing and his academic eminence; or by the number of committees of which he is a member, or by the size of his bank balance and the material possessions which he has amassed – but in the assessment of Jesus Christ these things are irrelevant. His assessment is quite simple – how many people has he helped?

Matthew 20: 20-28

A MISSIONARY tells a lovely story. She had been telling a class of African primary children about giving a cup of cold water in the name of Jesus. She was sitting on the verandah of her house. Into the village square came a company of native bearers. They had heavy packs. They were tired and thirsty, and they sat down to rest. Now they were men of another tribe, and had they asked the ordinary non-Christian native for water they would have been told to go and find it for themselves, because of the barrier between the tribes. But as the men sat wearily there, and as the missionary watched, from the school emerged a little line of tiny African girls. On their heads they had pitchers of water. Shyly and fearfully they approached the tired bearers, knelt and offered their pitchers of water. In surprise the bearers took them and drank and handed them back, and the girls took to their heels and ran to the missionary. 'We have given a thirsty man a drink,' they said, 'in the name of Jesus.' The little children took the story and the duty literally.

Would that more would do so! It is the simple kindnesses that are needed. As Mahomet said long ago, 'Putting a lost man on the right road, giving a thirsty man a drink of water, smiling in your brother's face – that too is charity'.

Mark 9: 41-42

NOT very many people have ever been argued into Christianity. Often our arguments do more harm than good. The only way to convince a man of the supremacy of Christ is to confront him with Christ. On the whole it is true to say that it is not argumentative and philosophical preaching and teaching which have won men for Christ; it is the presentation of the story of the Cross.

There is a story which tells how, towards the end of the nineteenth century, Aldous Huxley, the great agnostic, was a member of a house-party at a country house. Sunday came round, and most of the members prepared to go to church; but, very naturally, Huxley did not propose to go. Huxley approached a man known to have a simple and radiant Christian faith. He said to him: 'Suppose you don't go to church today. Suppose you stay at home and you tell me quite simply what your Christian faith means to you and why you are a Christian.' 'But,' said the man, 'you could demolish my arguments in an instant. I'm not clever enough to argue with you.' Huxley said gently: 'I don't want to argue with you; I just want you to tell me simply what this Christ means to you.' The man stayed at home and told Huxley most simply of his faith. When he had finished there were tears in the great agnostic's eyes. 'I would give my right hand,' he said, 'if only I could believe that.'

It was not clever argument that touched Huxley's heart. He could have dealt efficiently and devastatingly with any argument that that simple Christian was likely to have produced, but the simple presentation of Christ caught him by the heart. The best argument is to say to people: 'Come and see!' Of course, we have to know Christ ourselves before we can invite others to come to him. The true evangelist must himself have met Christ first.

John 1: 43-51

JESUS was no severe, austere killjoy. He loved to share in the happy rejoicing of a wedding feast.

There are certain religious people who shed a gloom wherever they go. They are suspicious of all joy and happiness. To them religion is a thing of black clothes, the lowered voice, the expulsion of social fellowship. It was said of Alice Freeman Palmer by one of her scholars: 'She made me feel as if I was bathed in sunshine.' Jesus was like that. C H Spurgeon, in his book *Lectures to my Students*, has some wise, if caustic, advice: 'Sepulchral tones may fit a man to be an undertaker, but Lazarus is not called out of his grave by hollow moans' .... 'I know brethren who, from head to foot, in garb, tone, manner, necktie and boots, are so utterly *parsonic* that no particle of manhood is visible .... Some men appear to have a white cravat twisted round their souls, their manhood is throttled with that starched rag' .... 'An individual who has no geniality about him had better be an undertaker and bury the dead, for he will never succeed in influencing the living' .... 'I commend cheerfulness to all who would win souls; not levity and frothiness, but a genial, happy spirit. There are more flies caught with honey than with vinegar, and there will be more souls led to heaven by a man who wears heaven in his face, than by one who bears Tartarus in his looks.'

Jesus never counted it a crime to be happy. Why should his followers do so?

John 2: 1-11

❖ ❖ ❖

THERE is another sense in which man's suffering shows what God can do. Affliction, sorrow, pain, disappointment, loss, always are opportunities for displaying God's grace.

First it enables the sufferer to show God in action. When trouble and disaster fall upon a man who does not know God, that man may well collapse; but when they fall on a man who walks with God, they bring out the strength and the beauty, and the endurance and the nobility, which are within a man's heart when God is there.

It is told that when an old saint was dying in an agony of pain, he sent for his family, saying: 'Come and see how a Christian can die.' It is when life hits us a terrible blow that we can show the world how a Christian can live, and, if need be, die. Any kind of suffering is an opportunity to demonstrate the glory of God in our own lives.

Second, by helping those who are in trouble or in pain, we can demonstrate to others the glory of God. Frank Laubach has the great thought that when Christ, who is the Way, enters into us – 'we become part of the Way. God's highway runs straight through us.'

When we spend ourselves to help those in trouble, in distress, in pain, in sorrow, in affliction, God is using us as the highway by which he sends his help into the lives of his people. To help a fellow-man in need is to manifest the glory of God, for it is to show what God is like.

John 9:1-5

ENEMIES

JESUS never asked us to love our enemies in the same way as we love our nearest and our dearest. The very word is different: to love our enemies in the same way as we love our nearest and our dearest would neither be possible nor right. This is a different kind of love.

Wherein does the main difference lie? In the case of our nearest and our dearest we cannot help loving them; we speak of *falling in love;* it is something which comes to us quite unsought; it is something which is born of the emotions of the heart. But in the case of our enemies, love is not only something of the *heart* – it is also something of the *will*. It is not something which we cannot help; it is something which we have to will ourselves into doing. It is in fact a victory over that which comes instinctively to the natural man.

Agapē does not mean a feeling of the heart, which we cannot help, and which comes unbidden and unsought; it means a determination of the mind, whereby we achieve this unconquerable goodwill even to those who hurt and injure us. *Agapē,* someone has said, is the power to love those whom we do not like and who may not like us. In point of fact we can only have *agapē* when Jesus Christ enables us to conquer our natural tendency to anger and to bitterness, and to achieve this invincible goodwill to all men.

It is then quite obvious that the last thing *agapē,* Christian love, means is that we allow people to do absolutely as they like, and that we leave them quite unchecked. No one would say that a parent really loves his child if he lets the child do as he likes. If we regard a person with invincible goodwill, it will often mean that we must punish him, that we must restrain him, that we must discipline him, that we must protect him against himself. But it will also mean that we do not punish him to satisfy our desire for revenge, but in order to make him a better man. It will always mean that all Christian discipline and all Christian punishment must be aimed, not at vengeance, but at cure. Punishment will never be merely retributive; it will always be remedial.

It must be noted that Jesus laid this love down as a basis for *personal relationships.* People use this passage as a basis for pacifism and as a text on which to speak about international relationships. Of course, it includes that, but first and foremost it deals with our personal relationships with our family and our neighbours and the people we meet with every day in life. It is very much easier to go about declaring that there should be no such thing as war between nation and nation, than to live a life in which we personally never allow any such thing as bitterness to invade our relationships with those we meet with every day. First and foremost, this commandment of Jesus deals with personal relationships. It is a commandment of which we should say first and foremost: 'This means me.'

We must note that this commandment is possible only for a Christian. Only the grace of Jesus Christ can enable a man to have this unconquerable benevolence and this invincible goodwill in his personal relationships with other people. It is only when Christ lives in our hearts that bitterness will die and this love spring to life. It is often said that this world would be perfect if only people would live according to the principles of the Sermon on the Mount; but the plain fact is that no one can even begin to live according to these principles without the help of Jesus Christ. We need Christ to enable us to obey Christ's command.

Lastly – and it may be most important of all – we must note that this commandment does not only involve allowing people to do as they like to us; it also involves that we should do something for them. *We are bidden to pray for them*. No man can pray for another man and still hate him. When he takes himself and the man whom he is tempted to hate to God, something happens. We cannot go on hating another man in the presence of God. The surest way of killing bitterness is to pray for the man we are tempted to hate.

Matthew 5: 43-48

FAITH

HERE is one of the great paradoxes. We are under the bounden duty of trying to understand our faith. But because we are finite and God is infinite, we can never fully understand. For that very reason a faith that can be neatly stated in a series of propositions, and neatly proved in a series of logical steps like a geometrical theorem, is a contradiction in terms. As G K Chesterton said, 'It is only the fool who tries to get the heavens inside his head, and not unnaturally his head bursts. The wise man is content to get his head inside the heavens.'

Even at our most intellectual, we must remember that there is a place for the ultimate mystery before which we can only worship, wonder and adore: 'How could I praise,/If such as I could understand?'

'I believe,' as Tertullian, a Christian writer of the third century, said, 'because it *is* impossible.'   *Mark 13: 3-6 and 21-23*

THEN comes the radiance of the supreme faith of Jesus. He says: 'I am not looking for honour in this world: I know that I will be insulted and rejected and dishonoured and crucified. But there is One who will one day assess things at their true value and assign to men their true honour; and he will give me the honour which is real because it is his.' Of one thing Jesus was sure – ultimately God will protect the honour of his own. In time Jesus saw nothing but pain and dishonour and rejection; in eternity he saw only the glory which he, who is obedient to God, will some day receive.

In the poem 'Paracelsus', Robert Browning wrote:

> ... *If I stoop*
> *into a dark tremendous sea of cloud,*
> *It is but for a time; I press God's lamp*
> *Close to my breast; its splendour, soon or late,*
> *Will pierce the gloom: I shall emerge one day.*

Jesus had the supreme optimism born of supreme faith, the optimism which is rooted in God. *John 8: 46-50*

FAMILY OF GOD

THE church is an empire in which all nations meet. Once a new church was being built. One of its great features was to be a stained glass window. The committee in charge searched for a subject for the window and finally decided on the lines of the hymn, 'Around the throne of God in heaven/Thousands of children stand'.

They employed a great artist to paint the picture from which the window would be made. He began the work and fell in love with the task. Finally he finished it. He went to bed and fell asleep, but in the night he seemed to hear a noise in his studio. He went into the studio to investigate; and there he saw a stranger with a brush and a palette in his hands working at his picture. 'Stop!' he cried. 'You'll ruin my picture!' 'I think,' said the stranger, 'that you have ruined it already.' 'How is that?' said the artist. 'Well,' said the stranger, 'you have many colours on your palette, but you have used only one for the faces of the children. Who told you that in heaven there were only children whose faces were white?' 'No one,' said the artist. 'I just thought of it that way.' 'Look!' said the stranger, 'I will make some of their faces yellow, and some brown, and some black, and some red. They are all there, for they have all answered my call.' '*Your* call?' said the artist. Who are you?' The stranger smiled. 'Once, long ago, I said, "Let the children come to me and don't stop them, for of such is the Kingdom of Heaven" – and I'm still saying it.' Then the artist realised that it was the Master himself, and as he did so the Master vanished from his sight. The picture looked so much more wonderful now with its black and yellow and red and brown children, as well as white.

In the morning the artist awoke and rushed through to his studio. His picture was just as he had left it; and he knew that it had all been a dream. Although that very day the committee was coming to examine the picture, he seized his brushes and his paints, and began to paint the children of every colour and of every race throughout all the world. When the committee arrived they thought the picture very beautiful and one whispered gently, 'Why! It's God's family at home.'

The church is the family of God; and that church which began in Palestine, small as the mustard seed, has room in it for every nation in the world. There are no barriers in the church of God. Man made barriers and God in Christ tore them down.

Mark 30-32

FATHER

IF we believe that God is Father, *it settles our relationship to God.* It is not that it removes the might, majesty and power of God. It is not that it makes God any the less God; but it makes that might, and majesty, and power, approachable for us.

There is an old Roman story which tells how an Emperor was enjoying a triumph. He had the privilege, which Rome gave to her great victors, of marching his troops through the streets of Rome, with all his captured trophies and prisoners in his train. So the Emperor was on the march with his troops. The streets were lined with cheering people. The tall legionaries lined the streets' edges to keep the people in their places.

At one point on the triumphal route, there was a little platform where the Empress and her family were sitting to watch the Emperor go by in all the pride of his triumph. On the platform with his mother there was the Emperor's youngest son – a little boy. As the Emperor came near, the little boy jumped off the platform, burrowed through the crowd, tried to dodge between the legs of a legionary, and to run out on to the road to meet his father's chariot.

The legionary stooped down and stopped him. He swung him up in his arms: 'You can't do that, boy,' he said. 'Don't you know who that is in the chariot? That's the Emperor. You can't run out to his chariot.' And the little lad laughed down: 'He may be your Emperor,' he said, 'but he's my father!'

That is exactly the way the Christian feels towards God. The might and the majesty and the power, are the might and the majesty and the power of one whom Jesus taught us to call *Our Father*.

Matthew 6: 9

❖ ❖ ❖

ABBA is the Aramaic word for *my father*. It is that one word which made all the difference. Jesus was not submitting to a God who made a cynical sport of men. Thomas Hardy finishes his novel *Tess of the D'Urbervilles,* after telling of her tragic life, with the terrible sentence, 'The President of the Immortals had finished his sport with Tess'. But Jesus was not submitting to a God who was an iron fate:

> But helpless pieces of the game he plays,
>   Upon this chequer board of nights and days,
>   Hither and thither moves and checks and slays –
> And one by one back in the closet lays.

God was not like that. Even in this terrible hour, when he was making this terrible demand, God was *father*.

When Richard Cameron, the covenanter, was killed, his head and hands were cut off by one Murray and taken to Edinburgh. 'His father being in prison for the same cause, the enemy carried them to him, to add grief unto his former sorrow, and inquired if he knew them. Taking his son's head and hands, which were very fair (being a man of a fair complexion like himself), he kissed them and said, "I know them – I know them. They are my son's – my own dear son's. It is the Lord. Good is the will of the Lord, who cannot wrong me nor mine, but hath made goodness and mercy to follow us all our days".'

If we can call God *father*, everything becomes bearable. Time and again we will not understand, but always we will be certain that 'the Father's hand will never cause his child a needless tear'. That is what Jesus knew. That is why he could go on – and it can be so with us.

Mark 14: 32

FOLLOW ME

JESUS – he never hesitated to tell men what they might expect, if they followed him. It is as if he said, 'Here is my task for you – at its grimmest and at its worst – do you accept it?' Plummer comments: 'This is not the world's way to win adherents.' The world will offer a man roses, roses all the way, comfort, ease, advancement, the fulfilment of his worldly ambitions. Jesus offered his men hardship and death. And yet the proof of history is that Jesus was right. In their heart of hearts men love a call to adventure.

After the siege of Rome in 1849, Garibaldi issued the following proclamation to his followers: 'Soldiers, all our efforts against superior forces have been unavailing. I have nothing to offer you but hunger and thirst, hardship and death; but I call on all who love their country to join with me' – and they came in their hundreds.

After Dunkirk, Winston Churchill offered his country 'blood, toil, sweat and tears'.

Prescott tells how Pizarro, that reckless adventurer, offered his little band the tremendous choice between the known safety of Panama, and the as yet unknown splendour of Peru. He took his sword and traced a line with it on the sand from east to west: 'Friends and comrades!' he said, 'on that side are toil, hunger, nakedness, the drenching storm, desertion and death: on this side, ease and pleasure. There lies Peru with its riches: here, Panama and its poverty. Choose each man what best becomes a brave Castilian. For my part I go south' – and he stepped across the line. And 13 men, whose names are immortal, chose adventures with him.

When Ernest Shackleton proposed his march to the South Pole, he asked for volunteers for that trek amidst the blizzards across the polar ice. He expected to have difficulty, but he was inundated with letters, from young and old, rich and poor, the highest and the lowest, all desiring to share in that great adventure.

It may be that the Church must learn again that we will never attract men to an easy way: it is the call of the heroic which ultimately speaks to men's hearts.   *Matthew 10: 16-22*

FORGIVENESS

WHEN Robert Louis Stevenson lived in the South Seas Islands, he used always to conduct family worship in the mornings for his household. It always concluded with the Lord's Prayer. One morning, in the middle of the Lord's Prayer, he rose from his knees and left the room. His health was always precarious, and his wife followed him thinking that he was ill. 'Is there anything wrong?' she said. 'Only this,' said Stevenson, 'I am not fit to pray the Lord's Prayer today.' No one is fit to pray the Lord's Prayer so long as the unforgiving spirit holds way within his heart. If a man has not put things right with his fellow men, he cannot put things right with God.   *Matthew 6: 12,14,15*

MODERN medicine would agree wholeheartedly that the mind can and does influence the physical condition of the body, and that a person can never have a healthy body when his mind is not in a healthy state.

Paul Tournier in *A Doctor's Case Book* quotes an actual example of that: 'There was, for example, the girl whom one of my friends had been treating for several months for anaemia, without much success. As a last resort my colleague decided to send her to the medical officer of the district in which she worked in order to get his permission to send her into a mountain sanatorium. A week later the patient brought word back from the medical officer. He proved to be a good fellow and he had granted the permit, but he added: "On analysing the blood, however, I do not arrive at anything like the figures you quote." My friend, somewhat put out, at once took a fresh sample of the blood, and rushed to his laboratory. Sure enough the blood count had suddenly changed. "If I had not been the kind of person who keeps carefully to laboratory routine," my friend's story goes on, "and if I had not previously checked my figures at each of my patient's visits, I might have thought that I had made a mistake." He returned to the patient and asked her, "Has anything out of the ordinary happened in your life since your last visit?" "Yes, something has happened," she replied. "I have suddenly been able to forgive someone against whom I bore a nasty grudge; and all at once I felt I could at last say, yes, to life!'" Her mental attitude was changed, and the very state of her blood was changed along with it. Her mind was cured, and her body was well on the way to being cured.   *Matthew 9: 1-8*

FELLOWSHIP

THERE is always a thrill in belonging to a noble company. Eric Linklater, the Scottish author, in his autobiography, tells of his experience in the disastrous March retreat in the First World War. He was with the Black Watch, and they had emerged from the battle with one officer, thirty men, and a piper, left of the battalion.

'The next day, marching peacefully in the morning light of France along a pleasant road, we encountered the tattered fragments of a battalion of the Foot Guards, and the piper, putting breath into his bag, and playing so that he filled the air like the massed bands of the Highland Division, saluted the tall Coldstreamers, who had a drum or two and some instruments of brass, that made also a gallant music. Stiffly we passed each other, swollen of chest, heads tautly to the rights, kilts swinging to the answer of the swagger of the Guards, and the Red Hackle in our bonnets, like the monstrance of a bruised but resilient faith. We were bearded and stained with mud. The Guards – the fifty men that were left of a battalion – were button-bright and clean shaved – we were a tattered and bedraggled crew from the coal mines of Fife and the back streets of Dundee, but we trod quick-stepping to the brawling tune of "Hielan Laddie", and suddenly I was crying with a fool's delight and the sheer gladness of being in such company.'

It is one of life's great thrills to have the sense of belonging to a goodly company and a goodly fellowship.

When Christianity costs something, we are closer than ever we were to the fellowship of Jesus Christ: and if we know the fellowship of his sufferings, we shall also know the power of his resurrection.

Matthew 10: 24-25

GOODNESS

IT is a man's characteristic that he is a mixture. James Boswell, in his *London Diary*, tells us how he sat in church enjoying the worship of God and yet at the same time was planning how to pick up a prostitute in the streets of London that same night.

The strange fact about man is that he is haunted both by sin and by goodness. Robert Louis Stevenson speaks about people 'clutching the remnants of virtue in the brothel or on the scaffold'. Sir Norman Birkett, the great QC and judge, speaks of the criminals he had defended and tried: 'They may seek to escape but they cannot; they are condemned to some nobility; all their lives long the desire for good is at their heels. the implacable hunter.'

Mark 6: 16-29

MOST people have an instinctive desire for goodness, but that desire is wistful and nebulous, rather than sharp and intense; and when the moment of decision comes they are not prepared to make the effort and sacrifice which real goodness demands. Most people suffer from what R L Stevenson called 'the malady of not wanting'. It would obviously make the biggest difference in the world if we desired goodness more than anything else.

When we approach this beatitude from that side, it is the most demanding, and indeed the most frightening, of them all. But not only is it the most demanding beatitude: in its own way it is also the most comforting. At the back of it there is the meaning that the man who is blessed is not necessarily the man who achieves this goodness, but the man who longs for it with his whole heart. If blessedness came only to him who achieved, then none would be blessed. But blessedness comes to the man who, in spite of failures and failings, still clutches to him the passionate love of the highest. As H G Wells somewhere said, 'A man may be a bad musician and yet be passionately in love with music'.

The true wonder of man is not that he is a sinner, but that even in his sin he is haunted by goodness, that even in the mud he can never wholly forget the stars. David had always wished to build the Temple of God: he never achieved that ambition; it was denied and forbidden him – but God said to him, 'You did well that it was in your heart' (I Kings 8:18). In his mercy God judges us, not only by our achievements, but also by our dreams. Even if a man never attains goodness, if to the end of the day he is still hungering and thirsting for it, he is not shut out from blessedness.

Matthew 5: 6

GIVING

ONE of the loveliest of all stories is that of *The Fourth Wise Man*. His name was Artaban. He set out to follow the star and he took with him a sapphire, a ruby and a pearl beyond price as gifts for the King. He was riding hard to meet his three friends, Caspar, Melchior and Balthasar, at the agreed place. The time was short; they would leave if he was late. Suddenly he saw a dim figure on the ground before him. It was a traveller stricken with fever. If he stayed to help he would miss his friends. He did stay; he helped and healed the man.

But now he was alone. He needed camels and bearers to help him across the desert because he had missed his friends and their caravan. He had to sell his sapphire to get them; and he was sad because the King would never have his gem.

He journeyed on and in due time came to Bethlehem, but again he was too late. Joseph and Mary and the baby had gone. Then there came the soldiers to carry out Herod's command that the children should be slain. Artaban was in a house where there was a little child. The tramp of the soldiers came to the door; the weeping of stricken mothers could be heard. Artaban stood in the doorway, tall and dark, with the ruby in his hand and bribed the captain not to enter. The child was saved; the mother was overjoyed – but the ruby was gone, and Artaban was sad because the King would never have his ruby.

For years he wandered looking in vain for the King. More that thirty years afterwards he came to Jerusalem. There was a crucifixion that day. When Artaban heard of Jesus being crucified, he sounded wondrous like the King and Artaban hurried towards Calvary. Maybe his pearl, the loveliest in all the world, could buy the life of the King. Down the street came a girl fleeing from a band of soldiers. 'My father is in debt,' she cried, 'and they are taking me to sell as a slave to pay the debt. Save me!' Artaban hesitated; then sadly he took out his pearl, gave it to one of the soldiers and bought the girl's freedom.

On a sudden the skies were dark; there was an earthquake and a flying tile hit Artaban on the head. He sank half-conscious to the ground. The girl pillowed his head on her lap. Suddenly his lips began to move. 'Not so, my Lord. For when saw I thee anhungered and fed thee? Or thirsty, and gave thee drink? When saw I thee a stranger, and took thee in? Or naked and clothed thee? When saw I thee sick in prison, and came unto thee? Thirty and three years have I looked for thee; but I have never seen thy face, nor ministered to thee, my King.' And then, like a whisper from very far away, there came a voice: 'Verily I say unto you, Inasmuch as thou hast done it unto one the least of these my brethren, thou hast done it unto me.' And Artaban smiled in death because he knew that the King had received his gifts.

The best way to use sacred things is to use them for men. It has been known for children to be barred from a church because that church was considered too ancient and sacred for such as they. It can be that a church is more concerned with the elaboration of its services than with the help of its simple folk and the relief of its poor. But the sacred things are only truly sacred when they are used for men. The shewbread was never so sacred as when it was used to feed a starving man. The Sabbath was never so sacred as when it was used to help those who needed help. The final arbiter in the use of all things is love and not law.

Mark 2: 23-28

GOD

MAN'S power over man is strictly limited to this life. A man can destroy another man's life *but not* his soul. In the 1914–18 War, the magazine *Punch* had a famous cartoon in which it showed the German Emperor saying to King Albert of Belgium, 'So now you have lost everything'; and back came Albert's answer, 'But not my soul!'

On the other hand, God's power is such that it can blot out a man's very soul. It is, therefore, only reasonable to fear God rather than to fear men. It was said of John Knox, as his body was being lowered into the grave, 'Here lies one who feared God so much that he never feared the face of man'.

Luke 12: 1-12

JESUS showed that he believed that there was a real kinship between earth and heaven. Jesus would not have agreed that 'earth was a desert drear'. He believed that in the ordinary, common, everyday things of life, men could see God. As William Temple put it: 'Jesus taught men to see the operation of God in the regular and the normal – in the rising of the sun and the falling of the rain and the growth of the plant.'

Long ago Paul had the same idea when he said that the visible world is designed to make known the invisible things of God (Romans 1: 20). For Jesus this world was not a lost and evil place: it was the garment of the living God. Sir Christopher Wren lies buried in St Paul's Cathedral, the great church that his own genius planned and built. On his tombstone there is a simple Latin inscription which means, 'If you wish to see his monument, look around you'. Jesus would have said, 'If you wish to see God, look around you'. Jesus finds in the common things of life a countless source of signs which lead men to God if they will only read them aright.

Mark 4: 3-9

❖   ❖   ❖

HOW, then, can we see God's *word*, God's *Logos*, God's *reason*, God's *mind* in the world in which we live?

We must look *outwards*. It was always a basic Greek thought that where there is order there must be a mind. When we look at the world we see an amazing order. The planets keep to their appointed courses. The tides observe their appointed times. Seed times and harvest, summer and winter, day and night, come in their appointed order. Clearly there is order in nature, and there-fore, equally clearly, there must be a mind behind it all. Further, that mind must be greater than any human mind because it achieves results that the human mind can *never* achieve.

No man can make day into night, or night into day; no man can make a living thing. If in the world there is order, there must be mind; and if in that order there are things which are beyond the mind of man to do, then the mind behind the order of nature must be a mind above and beyond the mind of man – and straightway we have reached God. To look outwards upon the world is to come face to face with the God who made it.

We must look *upwards*. Nothing demonstrates the amazing order of the universe so much as the movement of the world. Astronomers tell us that there are as many stars as there are grains of sand upon the seashore. If we may put it in human terms, think of the traffic problem of the heavens; and yet the heavenly bodies keep their appointed courses and travel their appointed way. An astronomer is able to forecast to the minute and to the inch when and where a certain planet will appear. An astronomer can tell us when and where an eclipse of the sun will happen hundreds of years from now, and he can tell us to the second how long it will last. It has been said that 'no astronomer can be an atheist'. When we look upwards, we see God.

We must look *inwards*. Where did we get the power to think, to reason and to know? Where did we get our knowledge of right and wrong? Why does even the most evil-ridden man know in his heart of hearts when he is doing a wrong thing? Kant, the German philosopher, said long ago that two things convinced him of the existence of God – the starry heavens above him and the moral law within him. We neither gave ourselves life, nor did we give ourselves the reason which guides and directs life. It must have come from some power outside ourselves. Where do remorse and regret and the sense of guilt come from? Why can we never do what we like and be at peace? When we look inwards, we find what the Roman Emperor Marcus Aurelius called 'the god within', and what Seneca called 'the holy spirit which sits within our souls'. No man can explain himself apart from God.

We must look *backwards*. Froude, the great historian, said that the whole of history is a demonstration of the moral law in action. Empires rise and empires collapse. As Kipling wrote: 'Lo, all our pomp of yesterday/Is one with Nineveh and Tyre!' And it is a demonstrable fact of history that moral degeneration and national collapse go hand in hand. 'No nation,' said George Bernard Shaw, 'has ever outlived the loss of its gods.'

So, even if Jesus Christ had never come into this world in bodily form, it would still have been possible for men to see God's *word,* God's *Logos,* God's *reason* in action. But although the action of the word was there for all to see, men never recognised him.

John 1: 10-11

HONESTY

NO ONE could ever say that he was induced to follow Jesus by false pretences. Jesus never tried to bribe men by the offer of an easy way. He did not offer men peace; he offered them glory. To tell a man he must be ready to take up a cross was to tell him he must be ready to be regarded as a criminal and to die.

The honesty of great leaders has always been one of their characteristics. In the days of the Second World War, when Sir Winston Churchill took over the leadership of the country, all that he offered men was 'blood, toil, tears and sweat'. Garibaldi, the great Italian patriot, appealed for recruits in these terms: 'I offer neither pay, nor quarters, nor provisions; I offer hunger, thirst, forced marches, battles and death. Let him who loves his country in his heart, and not with his lips only, follow me ... Soldiers, all our efforts against superior forces have been unavailing. I have nothing to offer you but hunger and thirst, hardship and death; but I call on all who love their country to join with me.'

Jesus never sought to lure men to him by the offer of an easy way; he sought to challenge them, to waken the sleeping chivalry in their souls, by the offer of a way than which none could be higher and harder. He came not to make life easy, but to make men great. *Mark 8: 31-33*

HOPE

SOMEONE has written the lines:

How I wish that there was some wonderful place
Called the Land of Beginning Again,
Where all our mistakes and all our heartaches
And all our poor selfish grief
Could be dropped like a shabby old coat at the door,
And never put on again.

In Jesus there is the gospel of the second chance. He was always intensely interested, not only in what a person had been, but also in what a person could be. He did not say that what they had done did not matter; broken laws and broken hearts always matter; but he was sure that every man has a future as well as a past. *John 7: 53; 8: 11*

❖ ❖ ❖

WE are living today in an atmosphere of despair. People despair of the church; they despair of the world; they look with shuddering dread on the future. 'Man,' said H G Wells, 'who began in a cave behind a windbreak, will end in the disease-soaked ruins of a slum.' Between the wars Sir Philip Gibbs wrote a book in which he looked forward, thinking of the possibility of a war of poison gas. He said something like this. 'If I smell poison gas in High Street, Kensington, I am not going to put on a gas-mask. I am going to go out and breathe deeply of it, because I will know that *the game is up.*'

So many people feel that for humanity the game is up. Now, no man can think like that *and* believe in God. If God is the God we believe him to be, there is no room for pessimism. There may be remorse, regret; there may be penitence, contrition; there may be heart-searching, the realisation of failure and of sin; but there can never be despair.

> *Workman of God! O lose not heart,*
> *But learn what God is like,*
> *And, in the darkest battle-field,*
> *Thou shalt know where to strike.*
>
> *For right is right, since God is God,*
> *And right the day must win:*
> *To doubt would be disloyalty,*
> *To falter would be sin.* Mark 4: 26-29

HYPOCRISY

T E LAWRENCE was a close personal friend of Thomas Hardy, the author. In the days when Lawrence was serving as an aircraftman in the Royal Air Force, he sometimes used to visit Hardy and his wife in his aircraftman's uniform. On one occasion his visit coincided with a visit of the Mayoress of Dorchester. She was bitterly affronted that she had to submit to meeting a common aircraftman, for she had no idea who he was. In French she said to Mrs Hardy that never in all her born days had she had to sit down to tea with a private soldier. No one said anything; then Lawrence said in perfect French: 'I beg your pardon, Madame, but can I be of any use as an interpreter? Mrs Hardy knows no French.' A snobbish and discourteous woman had made a shattering mistake because she judged by externals.

John 6: 41-51

❖　❖　❖

WE should examine the motives behind all our generosity. A man may give from a sense of duty:

He dropped a penny in the plate
And meekly raised his eyes,
Glad the week's rent was duly paid
For mansions in the skies.

We may give to God and to man much in the same way as we pay our income tax – as the satisfaction of a grim duty which we cannot escape.

A man may give purely from motives of self-interest. Consciously or unconsciously he may regard his giving as an investment. He may regard each gift as an entry on the credit side of his account in the ledger of God. Such giving, so far from being generosity, is rationalised selfishness.

A man may give in order to feel superior. Such giving can be a cruel thing. It can hurt the recipient much more than a blunt refusal. When a man gives like that, he stands on his little eminence and looks down. He may even with the gift throw in a short and smug lecture. It would be better not to give at all, than to give merely to gratify one's own vanity and one's own desire for power.

The Rabbis had a saying that the best kind of giving was

when the giver did not know to whom he was giving, and when the receiver did not know from whom he was receiving.

A man may give because he cannot help it. That is the only real way to give. The law of the kingdom is this – that if a man gives to gain reward, he will receive no reward; but if a man gives with no thought of reward, his reward is certain. The only real giving is that which is the uncontrollable outflow of love. Once Dr Samuel Johnson cynically described gratitude as 'a lively sense of favours to come'. The same definition could equally apply to certain forms of giving. God gave because he so loved the world – and so must we. *Luke 14: 12-14*

CATHERINE Carswell, in her autobiography *Lying Awake,* tells of her early days in Glasgow: 'The poor, one might say, were our pets. Decidedly they were always with us. In our particular ark we were taught to love, honour and entertain the poor.' The key-note, as she looked back upon it, was superiority and condescension. Giving was regarded as a duty, but often with the giving there was a moral lecture which provided a smug pleasure for the man who gave it.

In those days Glasgow was a drunken city on a Saturday night. She writes: 'Every Sunday afternoon, for some years, my father went a round of the cells of the police station, bailing out the weekend drunks with half-crowns, so that they might not lose their jobs on Monday morning. He asked each one to sign the pledge and to return his half-crown out of next week's wages.' No doubt he was perfectly right, but he gave from a smug eminence of respectability and included a moral lecture in the giving. He clearly felt himself to be in a quite different moral category from those to whom he gave.

It was said of a great, but superior man: 'With all his giving he never gives himself.' When a man gives, as it were, from a pedestal, when he gives always with a certain calculation, from a sense of duty, even a sense of Christian duty, he may give gener-ously of things, but the one thing he never gives is himself, and therefore the giving is incomplete. *Matthew 6: 2-4*

A NEEDY HEART

THE man who comes with no sense of need always misses the deepest meaning of scripture. When need awakens, the Bible is a new book. When Bishop Butler was dying he was troubled. 'Have you forgotten, my lord,' said his chaplain, 'that Jesus Christ is a saviour?' 'But,' said the dying bishop, 'how can I know that he is a saviour for me?' 'It is written,' said the chaplain, 'him that cometh unto me I will in nowise cast out.' And Butler answered, 'I have read these words a thousand times and I never saw their meaning until now. Now I die in peace.' The sense of need unlocked for him the treasury of scripture.

When we read God's book we must bring to it the open mind and the needy heart – and then to us also it will be the greatest book in the world. *Luke 6: 1-5*

HUMILITY

HUMILITY has always been one of the characteristics of great men. When Thomas Hardy, the novelist, was so famous that any newspaper would gladly have paid enormous sums for his work, he used sometimes to submit a poem, and always with it a stamped and addressed envelope for the return of his manuscript should it be rejected. Even in his greatness he was humble enough to think that his work might be turned down.

There are many stories and legends of the humility of Principal Cairns. He would never enter a room first. He always said, 'You first, I follow'. Once, as he came on to a platform, there was a great burst of applause in welcome. He stood aside and let the man after him come first and began himself to applaud. He never dreamed that the applause could possibly be for him; he thought it must be for the other man. It is only the little man who is self-important. *Luke 14: 7-11*

THERE is a tale of an old German schoolmaster who, when he entered his class of boys in the morning, used to remove his cap and bow ceremoniously to them. One asked him why he did this. His answer was: 'You never know what one of these boys may some day become.' He was right – because one of them was Martin Luther.   *John 6: 1-13*

❖   ❖   ❖

IT was in Bethlehem, David's city, that the Jews expected great David's greater Son to be born; it was there that they expected God's Anointed One to come into the world. And it was so.

The picture of the stable and the manger as the birthplace of Jesus is a picture indelibly etched in our minds; but it may well be that that picture is not altogether correct. Justin Martyr, one of the greatest of the early fathers, who lived about AD 150 and who came from the district near Bethlehem, tells us that Jesus was born in a cave near the village of Bethlehem (Justin Martyr: *Dialogue with Trypho* 78, 304); and it may well be that Justin's information is correct. The houses in Bethlehem are built on the slope of the limestone ridge; and it is very common for them to have a cave-like stable hollowed out in the limestone rock below the house itself; and very likely it was in such a cave-stable that Jesus was born.

To this day such a cave is shown in Bethlehem as the birth-place of Jesus, and above it the Church of the Nativity has been built. For very long that cave has been shown as the birthplace of Jesus. It was so in the days of the Roman Emperor Hadrian, for Hadrian, in a deliberate attempt to desecrate the place, erected a shrine to the heathen god Adonis above it. When the Roman Empire became Christian, early in the fourth century, the first Christian Emperor, Constantine, built a great church there, and that church, much altered and often restored, still stands.

H V Morton tells how he visited the Church of the Nativity in Bethlehem. He came to a great wall, and in the wall there was a door so low that he had to stoop to enter it; and through the door, and on the other side of the wall, there was the church.

Beneath the high altar of the church is the cave, and when the pilgrim descends into it he finds a little cavern about 14 yards long and four yards wide, lit by silver lamps. In the floor there is a star, and round it a Latin inscription: 'Here Jesus Christ was born of the Virgin Mary.'

When the Lord of Glory came to this earth, he was born in a cave where men sheltered the beasts. The cave in the Church of the Nativity in Bethlehem may be that same cave, or it may not be. That we will never know for certain. But there is something beautiful in the symbolism that the church where the cave is has a door so low that all must stoop to enter. It is supremely fitting that every man should approach the infant Jesus upon his knees.

Matthew 2: 1-2

IT will always remain true that a man's greatest glory is not what he has done, but what God has done for him. It might well be claimed that the discovery of the use of chloroform saved the world more pain than any other single medical discovery. Once someone asked Sir James Simpson, who pioneered its use, 'What do you regard as your greatest discovery?' – expecting the answer, 'Chloroform'. But Simpson answered, 'My greatest discovery was that Jesus Christ is my Saviour'.

Even the greatest man can say in the presence of God only,

Nothing in my hand I bring,
Simply to thy Cross I cling;
Naked, come to thee for dress:
Helpless, look to thee for grace;
Foul, I to the fountain fly;
Wash me, Saviour, or I die.

Pride bars from heaven; humility is the passport to the presence of God.

Luke 10: 17-20

INDIFFERENCE

NEGLECT can kill as much as persecution can. An author writes a book; it is sent out for review; some reviewers may praise it, others may damn it; it does not matter so long as it is noticed – the one thing which will kill a book stone dead is if it is never noticed at all for either praise or blame.

An artist drew a picture of Christ standing on one of London's famous bridges. He is holding out his hands in appeal to the crowds, and they are drifting past without a second look; only one girl – a nurse – gives him any response. Here we have the modern situation in so many countries today. There is no hostility to Christianity; there is no desire to destroy it; there is blank indifference. Christ is relegated to the ranks of those who do not matter. Indifference, too, is a sin, and the worst of all, for indifference kills.

It does not burn a religion to death; it freezes it to death. It does not behead it; it slowly suffocates the life out of it.

And so we are face to face with one great threatening truth – *it is also a sin to do nothing.* There are sins of action, sins of deed; but there is also a sin of inaction, and of absence of deeds. The sin of Chorazin, of Bethsaida, and of Capernaum, was the sin of doing nothing. Many a man's defence is: 'But I never did anything.' That defence may be in fact his condemnation.

Matthew 11: 20-24

❖   ❖   ❖

THERE is a fable which tells of three apprentice devils who were coming to this earth to finish their apprenticeship. They were talking to Satan, the chief of devils, about their plans to tempt and ruin men. The first said, 'I will tell them there is no God'. Satan said, 'That will not delude many, for they know that there is a God.' The second said, 'I will tell men there is no hell'. Satan answered, 'You will deceive no one that way; men know even now that there is a hell for sin'. The third said, 'I will tell men there is no hurry'. 'Go,' said Satan, 'and you will ruin them by the thousand.'

The most dangerous day in a man's life is when he learns that there is such a word as *tomorrow*. There are things which must not be put off, for no man knows if for him tomorrow will ever come.   *Matthew 24: 42-51*

INFLUENCE

MEN need to discover the lost radiance of the Christian faith. In a worried world, the Christian should be the only man who remains serene. In a depressed world, the Christian should be the only man who remains full of the joy of life. There should be a sheer sparkle about the Christian, but too often he dresses like a mourner at a funeral, and talks like a spectre at a feast. Wherever he is, if he is to be the salt of the earth, the Christian must be the diffuser of joy.

Jesus went on to say that if the salt had become insipid, it was fit only to be thrown out and trodden on by men. This is difficult, because salt does not lose its flavour and its saltness. E F F Bishop, in his book *Jesus of Palestine,* cites a very likely explanation given by Miss F E Newton. In Palestine the ordinary oven is out of doors and is built of stone on a base of tiles. In such ovens, 'in order to retain the heat, a thick bed of salt is laid under the tiled floor. After a certain length of time the salt perishes. The tiles are taken up, the salt removed and thrown on the road outside the door of the oven .... It has lost its power to heat the tiles and is thrown out'. That may well be the picture here.

But the essential point remains whatever the picture, and it is a point which the New Testament makes and remakes again and again – uselessness invites disaster. If a Christian is not fulfilling his purpose as a Christian, then he is on the way to disaster. We are meant to be the salt of the earth, and if we do not bring to life the purity, the antiseptic power, the radiance that we ought, then we invite disaster.   *Matthew 5:12*

THERE never was a time when this certainty was more needed than it is today. Geoffrey Heawood, headmaster of a great English public school, has written that the great tragedy and problem of this age is that we are standing at the crossroads, and the signposts have fallen down.

Beverley Nichols once wrote a book composed of interviews with famous people. One of the interviews was with Hilaire Belloc, one of the most famous of English Roman Catholics. After the interview Nichols wrote: 'I was sorry for Mr Belloc because I felt that he had nailed at least some of his colours to the wrong mast; but I was still sorrier for myself and for my own generation, because I knew that we had no colours of any kind to nail to the mast.'

We live in an age of uncertainty, an age when people have ceased to be sure of anything. Jesus was the herald of God, who came proclaiming the certainties by which men live; and we too must be able to say, 'I know whom I have believed'.

Matthew 9:35

IT will not happen very often, if at all, that anyone will slap us on the face, but time and time again life brings to us insults either great or small; and Jesus is here saying that the true Christian has learned to resent no insult and to see retaliation for no slight.

Jesus himself was called a gluttonous man and a wine-bibber. He was called the friend of tax-gatherers and harlots, with the implication that he was like the company he kept. The early Christians were called cannibals and incendiaries, and were accused of immorality, gross and shameless, because their service included the Love Feast.

When Lord Shaftesbury undertook the cause of the poor and the oppressed in the last century, he was warned that it would mean that 'he would become unpopular with his friends and people of his own class', and that 'he would have to give up all hope of ever being a cabinet minister'. When William Wilberforce began on his crusade to free the slaves, slanderous rumours that he was a cruel husband, a wife-beater, were deliberately spread abroad.

Time and time again in a church someone is 'insulted' because he is not invited to a platform party, or he is omitted from a vote of thanks, or in some way he does not get the place due to him. The true Christian has forgotten what it is to be insulted; he has learned from his Master to accept any insult, never to resent it, and never to seek to retaliate.   *Matthew 5:38-42*

JEALOUSY

JEALOUSY can distort our vision. William Shakespeare gave us the classic example of that in the tragedy of 'Othello'. Othello, the Moor, won fame by his heroic exploits and married Desdemona, who loved him with utter devotion and complete fidelity. As general of the army of Venice, Othello promoted Cassio and passed over Iago. Iago was consumed with jealousy. By careful plotting and the manipulation of facts, Iago sowed in Othello's mind the suspicion that Cassio and Desdemona were carrying on an intrigue. He manufactured evidence to prove it, and moved Othello to such a passion of jealousy that he finally murdered Desdemona by smothering her with a pillow.

A C Bradley writes: 'Such jealousy as Othello's converts human nature into chaos, and liberates the beast in man.'

Many a marriage and many a friendship have been wrecked on the rock of a jealousy which distorted perfectly innocent incidents into guilty actions, and which blinded the eye to truth and fact.   *Matthew 6:22-23*

JESUS

THERE is an unwritten saying of Jesus which never found its way into any of the gospels, but which rings true: 'Raise the stone and thou shalt find me; cleave the wood and I am there.' When the mason is working on the stone, when the carpenter is working with the wood, Jesus Christ is there. True happiness, true satisfaction, the sense of God, the presence of Christ – are all to be found in the day's work, when that day's work is honestly and conscientiously done.

Brother Lawrence, great saint and mystic, spent much of his working life in the monastery kitchen amidst the dirty dishes, and he could say, 'I felt Jesus Christ as close to me in the kitchen as ever I did at the blessed sacrament'.   *Matthew 13: 44*

ONCE Napoleon gave his verdict on Jesus. 'I know men,' he said, 'and Jesus Christ is more than a man.' Doubtless Peter could not have given a theological account and philosophic expression of what he meant when he said that Jesus was the Son of the living God; the one thing of which Peter was quite certain was that no merely human description was adequate to describe him.

This passage teaches that our discovery of Jesus Christ must be a *personal discovery*. Jesus' question is: '*You* — what do *you* think of me?' When Pilate asked him if he was the king of the Jews, his answer was: 'Do you say this of your own accord, or did others say it to you about me?' (John 18: 33,34).

Our knowledge of Jesus must never be at second hand. A man might know every verdict ever passed on Jesus; he might know every Christology that the mind of man had ever thought out; he might be able to give a competent summary of the teaching about Jesus of every great thinker and theologian — and still not be a Christian. Christianity never consists in *knowing about* Jesus; it always consists in *knowing Jesus*. Jesus Christ demands a personal verdict. He did not ask only Peter, he asks *every* man: 'You — what do you think of me?'

Matthew 16:13-16

THORWALDSEN, the great sculptor, once carved a statue of Jesus. He wished to see if the statue would cause the right reaction in those who saw it. He brought a little child to look at the statue and asked him: 'Who do you think that is?' The child answered: 'It is a great man.' Thorwaldsen knew that he had failed; so he scrapped his statue and began again. Again when he had finished, he brought the child and asked the same question: 'Who do you think that is?' The child smiled and answered: 'That is Jesus who said: "Let the children come to me."' Thorwaldsen knew that this time he had succeeded. The statue had passed the test of a child's eyes.

That is no bad test. George Macdonald once said that he placed no value on the alleged Christianity of a man at whose door, or at whose garden gate, the children were afraid to play. If a child thinks a person good, the likelihood is that he is good; if a child shrinks away, a man may be great but certainly he is not Christlike.

Somewhere J M Barrie draws a picture of a mother putting her little one to bed at night and looking down on him when he is half asleep, with an unspoken question in her eyes and in her heart: 'My child, have I done well today?' The goodness which can meet the clear gaze of a child and stand the test of a child's simplicity is goodness indeed. It was but natural that the children should recognise Jesus when the scholars were blind.

Matthew 21: 15-17

THE help which wins the approval of God is that which is given for nothing but the sake of helping.

Jesus confronts us with the wonderful truth that all such help given is given to himself, and all such help withheld is withheld from himself. How can that be? If we really wish to delight a parent's heart, if we really wish to move him to gratitude, the best way to do it is to help his child. God is the great Father; and the way to delight the heart of God is to help his children, our fellow men.

There were two men who found this parable blessedly true. The one was Francis of Asissi. He was wealthy and high-born and high-spirited; but he was not happy. He felt that life was incomplete. Then one day he was out riding and met a leper, loathsome and repulsive in the ugliness of his disease. Something moved Francis to dismount and fling his arms around this wretched sufferer; and in his arms the face of the leper changed to the face of Christ.

The other was Martin of Tours. He was a Roman soldier and a Christian. One cold winter day, as he was entering a city, a beggar stopped him and asked for alms. Martin had no money; but the beggar was blue and shivering with cold, and Martin gave what he had. He took off his soldier's coat, worn and frayed as it was; he cut it in two and gave half of it to the beggar man. That night he had a dream. In it he saw the heavenly places and all the angels and Jesus in the midst of them; and Jesus was wearing half of a Roman soldier's cloak. One of the angels said to him, 'Master, why are you wearing that battered old cloak? Who gave it to you?' And Jesus answered softly, 'My servant Martin gave it to me'.

When we learn the generosity, which without calculation helps men in the simplest things, we too will know the joy of helping Jesus Christ himself.   *Matthew 25: 31-46*

MANY of us still look for Jesus among the dead. There are those who regard him as the greatest man and the noblest hero who ever lived, as one who lived the loveliest life ever seen on earth; but who then died. That will not do. Jesus is not dead; he is alive. He is not merely a hero of the past; he is a living reality of the present.

> *Shakespeare is dust, and will not come*
> *To question from his Avon tomb,*
> *And Socrates and Shelley keep*
> *An Attic and Italian sleep.*
>
> *They see not. But, O Christians, who*
> *Throng Holborn and Fifth Avenue,*
> *May you not meet in spite of death,*
> *a traveller from Nazareth?*

There are those who regard Jesus simply as a man whose life must be studied, his words examined, his teaching analysed. There is a tendency to think of Christianity and Christ merely in terms of something to be studied. The tendency may be seen in the quite simple fact of the extension of the study group and the extinction of the prayer meeting. Beyond doubt study is necessary, but Jesus is not only someone to be studied: he is someone to be met and lived with every day. He is not only a figure in a book, even if that book be the greatest in the world: he is a living presence.

There are those who see in Jesus the perfect pattern and example. He is that; but a perfect example can be the most heart-breaking thing in the world. For centuries the birds gave men an example of flight, and yet not till modern times could man fly. Some of us when young were presented at school with a writing book. At the top it had a line of copperplate writing; below it had blank lines on which we had to copy it. How utterly discouraging were our efforts to reproduce that perfect pattern! But then the teacher would come and, with her hand, would guide our hand over the lines and we got nearer the ideal. That is what Jesus does. He is not only the pattern and the example; he helps us and guides us and strengthens us to follow the pattern and example. He is not simply a model for life; he is a living presence to help us to live.

It may well be that our Christianity has lacked an essential something because we too have been looking for him who is alive among the dead.   *Luke 24: 1-12*

JESUS came into the world to die. Holman Hunt has a famous picture of Jesus. It shows Jesus at the door of the carpenter's shop in Nazareth. He is still only a boy and has come to the door to stretch his limbs which had grown cramped over the bench. He stands there in the doorway with arms outstretched, and behind him, on the wall the setting sun throws his shadow, and it is the shadow of a cross. In the background there stands Mary, and as she sees that shadow there is the fear of coming tragedy in her eyes.

Jesus came into the world to live for men, and, in the end, to die for men. He came to give for men his life and his death.

Matthew 2: 9-12

WHEN Joseph and Mary were on their way to Egypt, the story runs, as the evening came they were very weary, and they sought refuge in a cave. It was very cold, so cold that the ground was white with hoar frost.

A little spider saw the baby Jesus and wished so much that he could do something to keep him warm in the cold night. He decided to do the only thing he could and spin his web across the entrance of the cave, to make, as it were, a curtain there.

Along the path came a detachment of Herod's soldiers, seeking for children to kill, to carry out Herod's bloodthirsty order. When they came to the cave they were about to burst in to search it, but their captain noticed the spider's web, covered with the white hoar frost and stretched right across the entrance to the cave. 'Look,' he said, 'at the spider's web there. It is quite unbroken and there cannot possibly be anyone in the cave, for anyone entering would certainly have torn the web.'

So the soldiers passed on, and left the holy family in peace, because a little spider had spun his web across the entrance to the cave. And that, so they say, is why to this day we put tinsel on our Christmas trees, for the glittering tinsel streamers stand for the spider's web, white with the hoar frost, stretched across the entrance to the cave on the way to Egypt. It is a lovely story, and this much, at least, is true – that no gift which Jesus receives is ever forgotten.   *Matthew 2: 13-15*

IN Palestine the ass was not a despised beast, but a noble one. When a king went to war he rode on a horse; when he came in peace he rode on an ass.

G K Chesterton has a poem in which he makes the modern donkey speak:

When fishes flew and forests walk'd
And figs grew upon thorn,
Some moment when the moon was blood
Then surely I was born.

With monstrous head and sickening cry
  And ears like errant wings,
The devil's walking parody
  Of all four-footed things.

The tatter'd outlaw of the earth
  Of ancient crooked will;
Starve, scourge, deride me, I am dumb,
  I keep my secret still.

Fools! For I also had my hour,
  One far fierce hour and sweet;
There was a shout about my ears,
  And palms before my feet.

It is a wonderful poem. Nowadays the ass is a beast of amused contempt, but in the time of Jesus it was the beast of kings. But we must note *what kind of a king Jesus was claiming to be*. He came meekly and lowly. He came in peace and for peace. They greeted him as the Son of David, but they did not understand.

When Jesus rode into Jerusalem that day, he claimed to be king, but he claimed to be King of peace. His action was a contradiction of all that men hoped for and expected.

Mark 11: 1-6

JUSTICE

JESUS begins by citing the oldest law in the world – an eye for an eye, a tooth for a tooth. That law is known as the *Lex Talionis*, and it may be described as the law of tit for tat.

It appears in the earliest known code of laws, the Code of Hammurabi, who reigned in Babylon from 2285-2242 BC. The principle is clear and apparently simple – if a man has inflicted an injury on any person, an equivalent injury shall be inflicted upon him.

The *Lex Talionis*, the law of tit for tat, so far from being a savage and bloodthirsty law, is in fact the *beginning of mercy*. Its original aim was definitely the *limitation of vengeance*. In the very earliest days the vendetta and the blood feud were characteristic of tribal society. If a man of one tribe injured a man of another tribe, then at once *all* the members of the tribe of the injured man were out to take vengeance on *all* the members of the tribe of the man who committed the injury; and the vengeance desired was nothing less than death. *This law deliberately limits vengeance.* It lays it down that only the man who committed the injury must be punished, and his punishment must be no more than the equivalent of the injury he has inflicted and the damage he has done. Seen against its historical setting, this is not a savage law, but a law of mercy.

So, then, ancient ethics were based on the law of tit for tat. It is true that that law was a law of mercy; it is true that it was a law for a judge and not for a private individual; it is true that it was never literally carried out; it is true that there were accents of mercy speaking at the same time. But Jesus obliterated the very principle of that law, because retaliation, however controlled and restricted, has no place in the Christian life.

Matthew 5: 38-42

THE KINGDOM OF GOD

NATURE'S growth is often *imperceptible*. If we see a plant every day, we cannot see its growth taking place. It is only when we see it, and then see it again after an interval of time, that we notice the difference. It is so with the Kingdom. There is not the slightest doubt that the Kingdom is on the way if we compare, not today with yesterday, but this century with the century which went before.

When Elizabeth Fry, the Quaker reformer, went to Newgate Prison in 1817, she found in the woman's quarters 300 women and numberless children crammed into two small wards. They lived and cooked and ate and slept on the floor. The only attendants were one old man and his son. They crowded, half-naked, almost like beasts, begging for money which they spent on drink at a bar in the prison itself. She found there a boy of nine who was waiting to be hanged for poking a stick through a window and stealing paints valued at twopence. In 1853 the weavers of Bolton were striking for a pay of seven and a half old pence a day; and the miners of Stafford were striking for a pay of two shillings and sixpence a week.

Nowadays things like that are unthinkable. Why? Because the Kingdom is on the way, the growth of the Kingdom may, like that of the plant, be imperceptible from day to day; but over the years it is plain.   *Mark 4: 26-29*

THERE will be surprises in the kingdom of God. Those who are very prominent in this world may have to be very humble in the next; those whom no one notices here may be the princes of the world to come.

There is a story of a woman who had been used to every luxury and to all respect. She died, and when she arrived in heaven an angel was sent to conduct her to her house. They passed many a lovely mansion and the woman thought that each one, as they came to it, must be the one allotted to her.

When they had passed through the main streets they came to the outskirts where the houses were much smaller; and on the very fringe they came to a house which was little more than a hut. 'That is your house,' said the conducting angel. 'What,' said the woman, 'that!? I cannot live in that.' 'I am sorry,' said the angel, 'but that is all we could build for you with the materials you sent up.'

The standards of heaven are not the standards of earth. Earth's first will often be last, and its last will often be first.

Luke 13: 22-30

❖ ❖ ❖

WORRY is not caused by external circumstances. In the same circumstances one man can be absolutely serene, and another man can be worried to death. Both worry and serenity come, not from circumstances, but from the heart.

Alistair MacLean, the bestselling novelist, quotes a story from Tauler, the German mystic. One day Tauler met a beggar. 'God give you a good day, my friend,' he said. The beggar answered, 'I thank God I never had a bad one.' Then Tauler said, 'God give you a happy life, my friend.' 'I thank God,' said the beggar, 'I am never unhappy.' Tauler in amazement said, 'What do you mean?' 'Well,' said the beggar, 'when it is fine, I thank God; when it rains, I thank God; and since God's will is my will, and whatever pleases him pleases me, why should I say I am unhappy when I am not?' Tauler looked at the man in astonishment. 'Who are you?' he asked. 'I am a king,' said the beggar. 'Where then is your kingdom?' asked Tauler. And the beggar answered quietly: *'In my heart.'*

Isaiah said it long ago: 'Thou dost keep him in perfect peace, whose mind is stayed on thee: because he trusts in thee' (Isaiah 26: 3). As the north-countywoman had it: 'I am always happy, and my secret is always to sail the seas, and ever to keep the heart in port.'

Matthew 6:25-41

KINSHIP

TRUE kinship lies in *a common interest*. The writer A M Chirgwin tells us a very interesting thing in *The Bible in World Evangelism*. One of the greatest difficulties that colporteurs and distributors of the Scriptures have is not so much to sell their books as to keep people reading them. He goes on: 'A colporteur in pre-Communist China had for years been in the habit of going from shop to shop and house to house. But he was often disappointed because many of his new Bible readers lost their zeal, until he hit upon the plan of putting them in touch with one another and forming them into a worshipping group which in time became a duly organized Church.' Only when these isolated units became part of a group which was bound together by a common interest, did real kinship come into being. Christians have that common interest because they are all people who desire to know more about Jesus Christ.

True kinship lies in *a common obedience*. The disciples were a very mixed group. All kinds of beliefs and opinions were mixed up among them. A tax-collector like Matthew and a fanatical nationalist like Simon the Zealot ought to have hated each other like poison, and no doubt at one time did. But they were bound together because both had accepted Jesus Christ as Master and Lord. Any platoon of soldiers will be made up of men from different backgrounds and from different walks of life and holding very different opinion; yet, it they are long enough together, they will be welded into a band of comrades because of the common obedience which they all share. Men can become friends of each other when they share a common master. Men can love each other only when they all love Jesus Christ.

True kinship lies in *a common goal*. There is nothing for binding men together like a common aim. Here there is a great lesson for the Church. Chirgwin, talking of renewed interest in the Bible, asks, does this 'point to the possibility of a new approach to the ecumenical problem based on biblical rather than on ecclesiastical considerations?' The Churches will never draw together so long as they argue about the ordination of their ministers, the form of Church government, the administration of the sacraments and all the rest of it. The one thing on which they can all come together is the fact that all of them are seeking to win men for Jesus Christ. If kinship comes from a common goal, then Christians above all men possess its secret, for all are seeking to know Christ better and to bring others within his Kingdom. Wherever else we differ, on that we can agree. *Mark 3: 31-35*

LEARNING

JESUS was walking by the lakeside; and as he walked he called Peter and Andrew, James and John. It is not to be thought that this was the first time he had seen them, or they him. As John tells the story, at least some of them were already disciples of John the Baptist (John 1: 35). No doubt they had already talked with Jesus and had already listened to him, but in this moment there came to them the challenge once and for all to throw in their lot with him.

The Greeks told how Xenophon first met Socrates. Socrates met him in a narrow lane and barred his path with his stick. First Socrates asked him if he knew where he could buy this and that, and if he knew where this and that were made. Xenophon gave the required information. Then Socrates asked him, 'Do you know where men are made good and virtuous?' 'No,' said the young Xenophon. 'Then,' said Socrates, 'follow me and learn!'

Jesus, too, called on these fishermen to follow him. It is interesting to note what kind of men they were. They were not men of great scholarship, influence, wealth, or social background. They were not poor, they were simple working people with no great background, and certainly, anyone would have said, with no great future. It was these ordinary men whom Jesus chose.

Once there came to Socrates a very ordinary man called Aeschines. 'I am a poor man,' said Aeschines. 'I have nothing else, but I give you myself.' 'Do you not see,' said Socrates, 'that you are giving me the most precious thing of all?'

What Jesus needs is ordinary folk who will give him themselves. He can do anything with people like that.

Matthew 4: 18-22

LIGHT

THE *light* Jesus brings is the *light* which puts chaos to flight. In the creation story God moved upon the dark, formless chaos which was before the world began and said, 'Let there be light'

(Genesis 1: 3). The new-created lights of God routed the empty chaos into which it came. So Jesus is *the light which shines in the darkness* (1: 5). He is the one person who can save life from becoming a chaos. Left to ourselves we are at the mercy of our passions and our fears.

When Jesus dawns upon life, light comes. One of the oldest fears in the world is the fear of the dark. There is a story of a child who was to sleep in a strange house. His hostess, thinking to be kind, offered to leave the light on when he went to bed. Politely he declined the offer. 'I thought,' said his hostess, 'that you might be afraid of the dark.' 'Oh, no,' said the lad, 'you see, it's God's darkness.'

With Jesus the night is light about us as the day.

John 1: 4

LISTENING TO GOD

WE must so heed God all our days that our sensitivity is never blunted, our awareness is never dimmed, our spiritual hearing never becomes spiritual deafness. It is a law of life that we will hear only what we are listening for and only what we have fitted ourselves to hear.

There is a story of a country man who was in the office of a city friend, with the roar of the traffic coming through the windows. Suddenly he said, 'Listen!'

'What is it?' asked the city man.

'A grasshopper,' said the country man.

Years of listening to the country sounds had attuned his ears to the country sounds, sounds that a city man's ear could not hear at all. On the other hand, let a silver coin drop, and the chink of the silver would have immediately reached the ears of the money-maker, while the country man might never have heard it at all.

Only the expert, the man who has made himself able to hear it, will pick out the note of each individual bird in the chorus of the birds. Only the expert, the man who has made himself able to hear it, will distinguish the different instruments in the orchestra and catch a lonely wrong note from the second violins.

It is the law of life that we hear what we have trained ourselves to hear; day by day we must listen to God, so that day by day God's voice may become, not fainter and fainter until we cannot hear it at all, but clearer and clearer until it becomes the one sound to which above all our ears are attuned.

Matthew 12: 31-33

H G WELLS once said that the voice of our neighbours sounds louder in our ears than the voice of God. The disciple is the man who has ceased to care what people say, because he thinks only of what God says. *John 8:31-32*

LOVE OF GOD

THE whole essence of Jesus' life is that in him we see clearly displayed the attitude of God to men. Now that attitude was the very reverse of what men had thought God's attitude to be. It was not an attitude of stern, severe, austere justice; not an attitude of continual demand. It was an attitude of perfect love, of a heart yearning with love and eager to forgive.

Let us use a human analogy. Lewis Hind, in one of his essays, tells us of the day that he discovered his father. He had always respected and admired his father; but he had always been more than a little afraid of him. He was in church with his father one Sunday. It was a hot drowsy day. He grew sleepier and sleepier. He could not keep his eyes open as the waves of sleep engulfed him. His head nodded, he saw his father's arm go up; and he was sure that his father was going to shake him or strike him. Then he saw his father smile gently and put his arm round his shoulder. He cuddled the lad to himself so that he might rest the more comfortably and held him close with the clasp of love. That day, Lewis Hind discovered that his father was not as he had thought him to be, and that his father loved him.

That is what Jesus did for men and for God. He literally brought men God's forgiveness upon earth. Without him they would never have even remotely known about it.

Mark 2: 7-12

❖ ❖ ❖

THERE are certain things which a man must face alone. Matthew Arnold, in his poem 'Isolation', speaks of …

This truth – to prove and make thine own:
Thou hast been, shalt be, art alone.

There are certain decisions which must be taken, and certain roads that must be walked, in the awful loneliness of a man's own soul. And yet, in the deepest sense of all, even in these times a man is not alone, for never is God nearer to him. Whittier, the American poet, writes of such a time,

Nothing before, nothing behind.
*   The steps of faith*
Fall on the seeming void, and find
*   The rock beneath.*

Here we see the essential loneliness of Jesus, a loneliness that was comforted by God.   *Mark 10: 32-34*

❖ ❖ ❖

ONCE Lincoln was asked how he was going to treat the rebellious southerners when they had finally been defeated and had returned to the Union of the United States. The questioner expected that Lincoln would take a dire vengeance, but he answered, 'I will treat them as if they had never been away'.

It is the wonder of the love of God that he treats us like that.

Luke 15: 11-32

THE word was already there at the very beginning of things. John's thought is going back to the first verse of the Bible. 'In the beginning God created the heavens and the earth' (Genesis 1: 1). What John is saying is this – the word is not one of the created things; the word was there before creation; the word is not part of the world which came into being in time; the word is part of eternity and was there with God before time and the world began. John was thinking of what is known as the pre-existence of Christ.

In many ways this idea of pre-existence is very difficult, if not altogether impossible, to grasp. But it does mean one very simple, very practical, and very tremendous thing. If the word was with God before time began, if God's word is part of the eternal scheme of things, it means that God was always like Jesus.

Sometimes we tend to think of God as stern and avenging; and we tend to think that something Jesus did changed God's anger into love and altered his attitude to men. The New Testament tells us, this passage of John especially, that God has always been like Jesus. What Jesus did was to open a window in time that we might see the eternal and unchanging love of God.

We may well ask, 'What then about some of the things that we read in the Old Testament? What abut the passages which speak about commandments of God to wipe out whole cities and to destroy men, women and children? What of the anger and the destructiveness and the jealousy of God that we sometimes read of in the older parts of Scripture?' The answer is this – it is not God who has changed; it is men's knowledge of him that has changed. Men wrote these things because they did not know any better; that was the stage which their knowledge of God had reached.

When a child is learning any subject, he has to learn it stage by stage. He does not begin with full knowledge; he begins with what he can grasp and goes on to more and more. When he begins music appreciation, he does not start with a Bach 'Prelude' and 'Fugue'; he starts with something much more simple; and goes through stage after stage until his knowledge grows. It was that way with men and God. They could only grasp and understand God's nature and his ways in part. It was only when Jesus came that they saw fully and completely what God has always been like.

It is told that a little girl was once confronted with some of the more bloodthirsty and savage parts of the Old Testament. Her comment was: 'But that happened before God became a Christian!'

If we may so put it with all reverence, when John says that the word was always there, he is saying that God was *always* a Christian. He is telling us that God was and is and ever shall be like Jesus; but men could never know and realise that until Jesus came.

John 1: 1-2

GREEK is a language which is rich in synonyms; its words often have shades of meaning which English does not possess. In Greek there are four different words for *love*.

There is the noun *storgē* with its accompanying verb *stergein*. These words are the characteristic words of *family love*. They are the words which describe the love of a parent for a child and a child for a parent. 'A child,' said Plato, '*loves* [*stergein*] and is loved by those who brought him into the world.' 'Sweet is a father to his children,' said Philemon, 'if he has *love* [*storgē*].' These words describe *family affection*.

There is the noun *erōs* and accompanying verb *eran*. These words describe the love of a man for a maid; there is always passion in them; and there is always sexual love. Sophocles, the Athenian poet, described *erōs* as 'the terrible longing'. In these words there is nothing essentially bad; they simply describe the passion of human love – but as time went on they began to be tinged with the idea of lust rather than love, and they never occur in the New Testament at all.

There is *philia* with its accompanying verb *philein*. These are the warmest and the best Greek words for love. They describe real love, real affection. *Hot philountes*, the present participle, is the word which describes a man's closest and nearest and truest friends. It is the word which is used in the famous saying of

Meander: 'Whom the gods *love,* dies young.' *Philein* can mean *to fondle* or *to kiss.* It is the word of warm, tender affection – the highest kind of love.

There is *agapē* with its accompanying verb *agapan. These words indicate unconquerable benevolence, invincible goodwill. (Agapē* is the word which is used here.) If we regard a person with *agapē,* it means that no matter what that person does to us, no matter how he treats us, no matter if he insults us or injures us or grieves us, we will never allow bitterness against him to invade our hearts, but will regard him with that unconquerable benevolence and goodwill which will seek nothing but his highest good.

Matthew 5: 43-48

WE do not believe in a mocking and a capricious God, or in a blind and iron determinism. Thomas Hardy finishes his novel *Tess of the d'Urbervilles* with the grim words: 'The President of the Immortals had ended his sport with Tess.' We believe in a God whose name is love. As Whittier had it:

> *I know not where His islands lift*
> > *Their fronded palms in air.*
> *I only know I cannot drift*
> > *Beyond His love and care.*

As Browning triumphantly declared his faith:

> *God, Thou art love! I build my faith on that …*
> *I know thee who has kept my path and made*
> *Light for me in the darkness, tempering sorrow*
> *So that it reached me like a solemn joy.*
> *It were too strange that I should doubt thy love.*

And as Paul had it: 'He who did not spare his own Son, but gave him up for us all, will he not also give us all things with him?' (Romans 8: 32).

No man can look at the Cross and doubt the love of God, and when we are sure of the love of God, it is easy to say, 'Thy will be done'.

Matthew 6: 10

❖ ❖ ❖

FOR Jesus no one is ever lost in the crowd, because Jesus is like God.

W B Yeats, the Irish lyric poet and dramatist, once wrote, in one of his moments of mystical beauty: 'The love of God is infinite for every human soul, because every human soul is unique; no other can satisfy the same need in God.' God gives all of himself to each individual person.

The world is not like that. The world is apt to divide people into those who are important and those who are unimportant.

In *A Night to Remember,* Walter Lord tells in detail the story of the sinking of the 'Titanic' in April 1912. There was an appalling loss of life, when that new and supposedly unsinkable liner hit an iceberg in the middle of the Atlantic. After the tragedy had been announced, the New York newspaper, *The American*, devoted a leader to it. The leader was devoted entirely to the death of John Jacob Astor, the millionaire; and at the end of it, almost casually, it was mentioned that 1800 others were also lost. The only one who really mattered, the only one with real news value, was the millionaire. The other 1800 were of no real importance.

Men can be like that, but God can never be like that. Bain, the psychologist, said in a very different connection that the sensualist has what he calls 'a voluminous tenderness'. In the highest and the best sense, there is a voluminous tenderness in God. James Agate said of G K Chesterton: 'Unlike some thinkers, Chesterton understood his fellow-men; the woes of a jockey were as familiar to him as the worries of a judge .... Chesterton, more than any man I have ever known, had the common touch. He would give the whole of his attention to a boot-black. He had about him that bounty of heart which men call kindness, and which makes the whole world kin.' That is the reflection of the love of God which allows no man to be lost in the crowd.

This is something to remember in a day and an age when the individual is in danger of getting lost. Men tend to become numbers in a system of social security; they tend as members of an association or union to almost lose their right to be individuals at all. W B Yeats said of Augustus John, the famous artist and portrait painter: 'He was supremely interested in the revolt from all that makes one man like another.'

To God one man is never like another; each is His individual child, and each has all God's love and all God's power at his disposal.   *Matthew 9: 20-22*

LOYALTY

THERE is always something thrilling in even being present on the great occasion, in being there when something memorable and crucial is happening. There is an even greater thrill in having a share, however small, in the actual action. That is the feeling about which Shakespeare wrote so unforgettably in his play 'Henry the Fifth', in the words he put into Henry's mouth before the battle of Agincourt:

> *He that shall live this day and see old age,*
> *Will yearly on the vigil feast his friends,*
> *And say, 'Tomorrow is Saint Crispin':*
> *Then will he strip his sleeve and show his scars,*
> *And say, 'These wounds I had on Crispin's day'.*
> ...   .
> *And gentlemen in England now a-bed*
> *Shall think themselves accurs'd they were not here,*
> *And hold their manhoods cheap while any speaks*
> *That fought with us upon Saint Crispin's day.*

When a man is called on to suffer something for his Christianity, that is always a crucial moment; it is the great occasion; it is the clash between the world and Christ; it is a moment in the drama of eternity. To have a share in such a moment is not a penalty but a glory. 'Rejoice at such a moment,' says Jesus; 'and be glad.'   *Matthew 5: 10-12*

MAN

MAN *was born for greatness.* 'God created man in His own image, in the image of God He created him' (Genesis 1: 27). God said: 'Let us make man in our image, after our likeness' (Genesis 1: 26). Man was created in the image of God. God's dream for man was a dream of greatness. Man was designed for fellowship with God. He was created that he might be nothing less than kin to God. As Cicero, the Roman thinker, saw it: 'The only difference between man and God is in point of time.' Man was essentially man born to be king.

Man lost his greatness. Instead of being the servant of God, man became the slave of sin. As G K Chesterton said: 'Whatever else is true of man, man is not what he was meant to be.' He used his free-will to defy and to disobey God, rather than to enter into friendship and fellowship with him. Left to himself man had frustrated the design and plan of God in His creation.

Matthew 1: 1-17

MALADY OF NOT WANTING

ROBERT Louis Stevenson, in *The Master of Ballantrae,* draws a picture of the master leaving the ancestral home of Durrisdeer for the last time. Even he is sad. He is talking to the faithful family steward.

'Ah! McKellar,' he said. 'Do you think I have never a regret?'

'I do not think,' said McKellar, 'that you could be so bad a man unless you had all the machinery for being a good one.'

'Not all,' said the master, 'not all. It is there you are in error. *The malady of not wanting.*'

It was the malady of not wanting enough which meant tragedy for the man who came running to Jesus. It is the malady from which most of us suffer. We all want goodness, but so few of us want it enough to pay the price.

Mark 10: 17-22

MARY'S SON

THE basic trouble in the human situation is that men wish to do as little as possible and to get as much as possible. It is only when they are filled with the desire to put into life more than they take out, that life for themselves and for others will be happy and prosperous. Rudyard Kipling has a poem called 'Mary's Son', which is advice on the spirit in which a man must work:

If you stop to find out what your wages will be
And how they will clothe and feed you,
Willie, my son, don't you go to the Sea,
For the Sea will never need you.

If you ask for the reason of every command,
And argue with people about you,
Willie, my son, don't you go on the Land,
For the Land will do better without you.

If you stop to consider the work that you've done
And to boast what your labour is worth, dear,
Angels may come for you, Willie, my son,
But you'll never be wanted on earth dear!

Mark 10: 41-45

INSTINCTIVELY Mary turned to Jesus whenever something went wrong. She knew her son. It was not till he was thirty years old that Jesus left home; and all these years Mary lived with him. There is an old legend which tells of the days when Jesus was a little baby in the home in Nazareth. It tells how in those days when people felt tired and worried and hot and bothered and upset, they would say: 'Let us go and look at Mary's child', and they would go and look at Jesus, and somehow all their troubles rolled away. It is still true that those who know Jesus intimately instinctively turn to him when things go wrong – and they never find him wanting.

John 2: 1-11

MARTYRDOM

WE do well to remember that, while we are bound to accept martyrdom for our faith, we are forbidden to court martyrdom. If suffering for the faith comes to us in the course of duty, it must be accepted; but it must not be needlessly invited – to invite it does more harm than good to the faith we bear. The self-constituted martyr is much too common in all human affairs.

It has been said that there is sometimes more heroism in daring to fly from danger than in stopping to meet it. There is real wisdom in recognising when to escape.

André Maurois, in *Why France Fell,* tells of a conversation he had with Winston Churchill. There was a time at the beginning of the Second World War when Great Britain seemed strangely inactive and unwilling to act. Churchill said to Maurois: 'Have you observed the habits of lobsters?' 'No,' answered Maurois to this somewhat surprising question. Churchill went on: 'Well, if you have the opportunity, study them. At certain periods in his life the lobster loses his protective shell. At this moment of moulting even the bravest crustacean retires into a crevice in the rock, and waits patiently until a new carapace has time to grow. As soon as this new armour has grown strong, he sallies out of the crevice, and becomes once more a fighter, lord of the seas. England, through the faults of imprudent ministers, has lost its carapace; we must wait in our crevice until the new one has time to grow strong.' This was a time when inaction was wiser than action; and when to escape was wiser than to attack.

If a man is weak in the faith, he will do well to avoid disputations about doubtful things, and not to plunge into them. If a man knows that he is susceptible to a certain temptation, he will do well to avoid the places where that temptation will speak to him, and not to frequent them. If a man knows that there are people who anger and irritate him, and who bring the worst out of him, he will be wise to avoid their society, and not to seek it. Courage is not recklessness; there is no virtue in running needless risks. God's grace is not meant to protect the foolhardy, but the prudent. *Matthew 10: 23*

NEEDS OF OTHERS

DIOGENES was one of the great teachers of ancient Greece. He was a man who loved virtue, and a man with a caustic tongue. He was never tired of comparing the decadence of Athens — where he spent most of his time — with the strong simplicities of Sparta. One day someone said to him: 'If you think so much of Sparta and so little of Athens, why don't you leave Athens and go and stay in Sparta?' His answer was, 'Whatever I may wish to do, I must stay where men need me most'. It was sinners who needed Jesus, and amongst sinners he would move.

When Jesus said, 'I came not to call the righteous, but sinners', we must understand what he was saying. He was not saying that there were some people who were so good they had no need of anything which he could give; still less was he saying he was not interested in people who were good. This is a highly compressed saying. Jesus was saying: 'I did not come to invite people who are so self-satisfied that they are convinced they do not need anyone's help; I came to invite people who are very conscious of their sin and desperately aware of their need for a saviour.'

He was saying: 'It is only those who know how much they need me who can accept my invitation.'   *Matthew 9: 10-13*

NOWHERE

J H WITHERS quotes a saying from Gerald Healy's play 'The Black Stranger'. The scene is in Ireland, in the terrible days of famine in the mid-nineteenth century. For want of something better to do, and for lack of some other solution, the government had set men to digging roads to no purpose and to no destination. Michael finds out about this. He comes home one day and says in poignant wonder to his father, 'They're makin' roads that lead to nowhere'.

If we believe in prophecy, that is what we can never say. History can never be a road that leads to nowhere. We may not use prophecy in the same way as our fathers did, but at the back of the fact of prophecy lies the eternal fact that life and the world are not on the way to nowhere, but on the way to the goal of God.   *Matthew 1: 1-17*

OBEDIENCE

KNOWLEDGE only becomes relevant when it is translated into action. It would be perfectly possible for a man to pass an examination in Christian Ethics with the highest distinction, and yet not to be a Christian. Knowledge must become action; theory must become practice; theology must become life. There is little point in going to a doctor, unless we are prepared to do the things we hear him say to us. There is little point in going to an expert, unless we are prepared to act upon his advice. And yet there are thousands of people who listen to the teaching of Jesus Christ every Sunday, and who have a very good knowledge of what Jesus taught, and who yet make little or no deliberate attempt to put it into practice. If we are to be in any sense followers of Jesus we must *hear* and *do*.

Is there any word in which *hearing* and *doing* are summed up? There is such a word – and that word is *obedience*. Jesus demands our implicit obedience. To learn to obey is the most important thing in life.

Some time ago there was a report of the case of a sailor in the Royal Navy who was very severely punished for a breach of discipline. So severe was the punishment that in certain civilian quarters it was thought to be far too severe. A newspaper asked its readers to express their opinions about the severity of the punishment.

One who answered was a man who himself had served for years in the Royal Navy. In his view the punishment was not too severe. He held that discipline was absolutely essential, for the purpose of discipline was to condition a man automatically and unquestioningly to obey orders, and on such obedience a man's life might well depend.

He cited a case from his own experience. He was in a launch which was towing a much heavier vessel in a rough sea. The vessel was attached to the launch by a wire hawser. Suddenly, in the midst of the wind and the spray, there came a single, insistent word of command from the officer in charge of the launch – 'Down!' he shouted. On the spot, the crew flung themselves down. Just at that moment the wire towing hawser snapped, and the broken parts of it whipped about like a maddened steel snake. If any man had been struck by it he would have been instantly killed. But the whole crew automatically obeyed and no one was injured. If anyone had stopped to argue, or ask why, he would have been a dead man. Obedience saved lives.

It is such obedience that Jesus demands. It is Jesus' claim that obedience to him is the only sure foundation for life; and it is his promise that the life which is founded on obedience to him is safe, no matter what storms may come.   *Matthew 7: 24-27*

OPPORTUNITIES LOST

IT is one of the great basic facts of life that time and time again an opportunity comes to a man − and does not come back. To those people in Palestine there was coming the opportunity to receive the Gospel, but if they did not take it, the opportunity might well never return. As the proverb has it: 'Three things come not back − the spoken word, the spent arrow, and the lost opportunity.'

This happens in every sphere of life. In his autobiography, *Chiaroscuro,* Augustus John tells of an incident and adds a laconic comment. He was in Barcelona: 'It was time to leave for Marseilles. I had sent forward my baggage and was walking to the station, when I encountered three Gitanas engaged in buying flowers at a booth. I was so struck by their beauty and flashing elegance that I almost missed my train. Even when I reached Marseilles and met my friend, this vision still haunted me, and I positively had to return. But I did not find these gypsies again. *One never does.*'

The artist was always looking for glimpses of beauty to transfer to his canvas − but he knew well that if he did not paint the beauty when he found it, all the chances were that he would never catch that glimpse again. The tragedy of life is so often the tragedy of the lost opportunity.   *Matthew 10: 11-15*

❖   ❖   ❖

HERE is the tragedy of a people being prepared for a task and then refusing that task.

It may be that parents plan and save and sacrifice to give a son or a daughter a chance in life, to prepare that son or daughter for some special task and opportunity – and then, when the chance comes, the one for whom so much sacrifice was made refuses to grasp the opportunity, or fails miserably when confronted with the challenge. Therein is tragedy. And that is what happened to God.

It would be wrong to think God prepared only the Jewish people. God is preparing every man and woman and child in this world for some task that he has in store for them. A novelist tells of a girl who refused to touch the soiling things of life. When she was asked why, she said: 'Some day something fine is going to come into my life, and I want to be ready for it.' The tragedy is that so many people refuse the task God has for them.

We may put it in another way – a way that strikes home – there are so few people who become what they have it in them to be. It may be through lethargy and laziness, it may be through timidity and cowardice, it may be through lack of discipline or through self-indulgence, it may be through involvement in second-bests and byways; but the world is full of people who have never realised the possibilities which are in them.

We need not think of the task God has in store for us in terms of some great act or achievement of which all men will know. It may be to fit a child for life; it may be at some crucial moment to speak that word and exert that influence which will stop someone ruining his life; it may be to do some quite small job superlatively well; it may be to touch the lives of many by our hands, our voices or our minds. The fact remains that God is preparing us, by all the experiences of life, for *something;* and many refuse the task when it comes and never even realise that they are refusing it.

There is all the pathos in the world in the simple saying: 'He came to his own home – and his own people gave him no welcome.' It happened to Jesus long ago – and it is happening yet.

John 1: 10-11

OUR LIVES

NO man can tell the day or the hour when eternity will invade time and summons will come. How, then, would we like God to find us?

We would like him to find us *with our work completed*. Life, for so many of us, is filled with loose ends. There are things undone and things half done; things put off and things not even attempted. Great men have always the sense of a task that must be finished. The English lyric poet Keats wrote:

> *When I have fears that I may cease to be*
> *Before my pen has glean'd my teeming brain.*

Robert Louis Stevenson wrote:

> *When morning drum-call on my eager ear*
> *Thrills unforgotten yet; the morning dew*
> *Lies yet undried along my field of noon.*
>
> *But now I pause at whiles in what I do,*
> *And count the bell, and tremble lest I hear*
> *(My work untrimmed) the sunset gun too soon.*

Jesus himself said: 'I have accomplished the work which thou gavest me to do' (John 17: 4). No man should ever lightly leave undone a task he ought to have finished, before night falls.

Luke 12: 35-48

WE run a certain danger. It is easy to think that, once we have made a commitment of ourselves to Jesus Christ, we have reached the end of the road and can sit back as if we had achieved our goal. There is no such finality in the Christian life. A man must ever be going forward or necessarily he goes backward.

The Christian way is like a climb up a mountain pathway

towards a peak which will never be reached in this world. It was said of two gallant climbers who died on Mount Everest: 'When last seen they were going strong for the top.' It was inscribed on the grave of an Alpine guide who had died on the mountain-side: 'He died climbing.' For the Christian, life is ever an upward and an onward way.   *Luke 13: 22-30*

❖   ❖   ❖

ALL his life William Wilberforce, who freed the slaves, was a little, insignificant, ailing creature. When he rose to address the House of Commons, the members at first used to smile at this queer little figure; but as the fire and the power came from the man, they used to crowd the benches whenever he rose to speak. As it was put: 'The little minnow became a whale.' His message, his task, the flame of truth and the dynamic of power conquered his physical weakness.

There is a picture of John Knox preaching in his old age. He was a done old man; he was so weak that he had to be half lifted up the pulpit steps and left supporting himself on the book-board; but before he had long begun his sermon the voice had regained its old trumpet-call and he was like 'to ding the pulpit into blads [to knock the pulpit into splinters] and leap out of it'. The message filled the man with a kind of supernatural strength.   *John 4: 31-34*

❖   ❖   ❖

JESUS claims that he came that men might have life, and might have it more abundantly. The Greek phrase used for *having it more abundantly* means to have a *superabundance of a thing*. To be a follower of Jesus, to know who he is and what he means, is to have a superabundance of life.

A Roman soldier came to Julius Caesar with a request for permission to commit suicide. He was a wretched, dispirited creature with no vitality. Caesar looked at him. 'Man,' he said, 'were you ever really alive?'

When we try to live our own lives, life is a dull, dispirited thing. When we walk with Jesus, there comes a new vitality, a superabundance of life. It is only when we live with Christ that life becomes really worth living and we begin to live in the real sense of the word.

John 10: 7-10

❖ ❖ ❖

THE penalty of being a man is to have a split personality. In human nature the beast and the angel are strangely intermingled.

It is told that once Schopenhauer, the gloomy philosopher, was found wandering. He was asked, 'Who are you?'

'I wish you could tell me,' he answered.

Robert Burns said of himself: 'My life reminded me of a ruined temple. What strength, what proportion in some parts! What unsightly gaps, what prostrate ruins in others!'

Man's trouble has always been that he is haunted both by sin and by goodness. The coming of Jesus unifies that disintegrated personality into one. He finds victory over his warring self by being conquered by Jesus Christ.

Mark 1: 14-15

❖ ❖ ❖

NO ploughman ever ploughed a straight furrow looking back over his shoulder. There are some whose hearts are in the past. They walk forever looking backwards and thinking wistfully of the good old days.

Watkinson, the great preacher, tells how once, at the seaside, when he was with his little grandson, he met an old minister. The old man was very disgruntled and, to add to all his troubles, he had a slight touch of sun-stroke. The little boy had been listening but had not picked it up quite correctly; and when they left the grumbling complaints of the old man, he turned to Watkinson and said, 'Grandad, I hope *you* never suffer from a *sunset*'.

The Christian marches on, not to the sunset, but to the dawn. The watchword of the kingdom is not 'backwards!', but *'forwards!'*

Luke 9: 57-62

PARENTS

JESUS was growing up to boyhood, and then to manhood, in a good home; and there can be no greater start to life than that.

J S Blackie, the famous Edinburgh professor, once said in public, 'I desire to thank God for the good stock-in-trade, so to speak, which I inherited from my parents for the business of life'.

George Herbert, the seventeenth century English poet, once said, 'A good mother is worth a hundred schoolmasters'.

So, for Jesus, the years passed, silently but mouldingly, in the circle of a good home.

Jesus was fulfilling the duties of an eldest son. It seems most likely that Joseph died before the family had grown up. Maybe he was already much older than Mary when they married. In the story of the Wedding Feast at Cana of Galilee there is no mention of Joseph, although Mary is there, and it is natural to suppose that Joseph had died.

So Jesus became the village craftsman of Nazareth to support his mother and his younger brothers and sisters. A world was calling him, and yet he first fulfilled his duty to his mother and to his own folks and to his own home.

When his mother died, Sir James Barrie could write: 'I can look back, and I cannot see the smallest thing undone.' There lies happiness. It is on those who faithfully and ungrudgingly accept the simple duties that the world is built.

One of the great examples of this is the great doctor, Sir James Young Simpson, the discoverer of chloroform. He came from a poor home. One day his mother took him on her knee and began to darn his stockings. When she had finished, she looked at her neat handiwork. 'My Jamie,' she said, 'mind when your mither's awa' that she was a grand darner.'

'Jamie' was the 'wise wean, the little box of brains', and his family knew it. They had their dreams for him. His brother Sandy said, 'I aye felt he would be great some day'. And so, without jealousy and willingly, his brothers worked in the bakeshop and at their jobs that the lad might have his college education and his chance. There would have been no Sir James Simpson had there not been simple folk willing to do simple things and to deny themselves, so that the brilliant lad might have his chance.

Jesus is the great example of one who accepted the simple duties of the home. *Matthew 2: 23 - 3: 1*

THE PAST

WE must never look on life as a kind of battle between the past and the present. The present grows out of the past.

After Dunkirk, in the Second World War, there was a tendency on all hands to look for someone to blame for the disaster which had befallen the British forces, and there were many who wished to enter into bitter recriminations with those who had guided things in the past. At that time Mr Winston Churchill, as he then was, said a very wise thing: 'If we open a quarrel between the past and the present, we shall find that we have lost the future.'

There had to be the Law before the Gospel could come. Men had to learn the difference between right and wrong; men had to learn their own human inability to cope with the demands of the law, and to respond to the commands of God; men had to learn a sense of sin and unworthiness and inadequacy.

Men blame the past for many things – and often rightly – but it is equally, and even more necessary, to acknowledge our debt to the past. As Jesus saw it, it is man's duty neither to forget nor to attempt to destroy the past, but to build upon the foundation of the past. We have entered into other men's labours, and we must so labour that other men will enter into ours.

Matthew 5: 17-20

WORRY cannot affect the past, for the past is past. The Persian poet Omar Khayyam was grimly right:

The moving finger writes, and having writ,
Moves on; nor all thy piety nor wit,
Shall lure it back to cancel half a line,
Nor all thy tears wash out a word of it.

The past is past. It is not that a man can, or ought, to disso-
ciate himself from his past; but he ought to use his past as a
spur and a guide for better action in the future, and not as something about which he broods until he has worried himself into
a paralysis of action.   *Matthew 6: 25-34*

PEOPLE

JESUS' first followers were simple folk. They did not come from
the schools and the colleges; they were not drawn from the
ecclesiastics or the aristocracy; they were neither learned nor
wealthy. They were fishermen. That is to say, they were ordinary
people. No one ever believed in the ordinary man as Jesus did.

Once George Bernard Shaw said, 'I have never had any feeling for the working-classes, except a desire to abolish them, and
replace them by sensible people'. In *The Patrician,* John Galsworthy
makes Miltoun, one of the characters, say, 'The mob! How I
loathe it! I hate its mean stupidity, I hate the sound of its voice,
and the look on its face – it's so ugly, so little!' Once, in a fit of
temper, Thomas Carlyle declared that there were 27 millions of
people in England – mostly fools!

Jesus did not feel like that. Abraham Lincoln said: 'God must
love the common people – he made so many of them.' It was as
if Jesus said, 'Give me twelve ordinary men and with them, if
they will give themselves to me, I will change the world'.

A man should never think so much of what he is, as of what
Jesus Christ can make him.   *Mark 1: 16-20*

IN this country we are, to this day, suffering in the world of
industrial relationships from the fact that in the days of the
Industrial Revolution people were treated as things.

Sir Arthur Bryant, in *English Saga,* tells of some of the things which happened in those days. Children of seven and eight years of age – there is actually a case of a child of three – were employed in the mines. Some of them dragged trucks along galleries on all fours; some of them pumped out water, standing knee deep in the water for twelve hours a day; some of them, called trappers, opened and shut the ventilating doors of the shafts, and were shut into little ventilating chambers for as much as 16 hours a day.

In 1815 children were working in the mills from five in the morning until eight at night, without even a Saturday half-holiday, and with half an hour off for breakfast and half an hour off for dinner. In 1833 there were 84,000 children under 14 in the factories.

There is *actually* a case recorded in which the children, whose labour was no longer required, were taken to a common and turned adrift. The owners objected to the expression 'turned adrift'. They said that the children had been set at liberty. They agreed that the children might find things hard: 'They would have to beg their way or something of that sort.'

In 1842 the weavers of Burnley were being paid the equivalent of 4p a day, and the miners of Staffordshire 15p a day.

There were those who saw the criminal folly of all this. Thomas Carlyle thundered: 'If the cotton industry is founded on the bodies of rickety children, it must go; if the devil gets in your cotton-mill, shut the mill.'

It was pleaded that cheap labour was necessary to keep costs down. Samuel Taylor Coleridge answered: 'You talk about making this article cheaper by reducing its price in the market from 4p to 3p. But suppose in so doing you have rendered your country weaker against a foreign foe; suppose you have demoralised thousands of your fellow-countrymen, and have sown discontent between one class of society and another, your article is tolerably dear, I take it, after all.'

It is perfectly true that things are very different nowadays. But there is such a thing as racial memory. Deep in the unconscious memory of people, the impression of these bad days is indelibly impressed. Whenever people are treated as things, as machines, as instruments for producing so much labour and for enriching those who employ them, then as certainly as night follows day, disaster follows. A nation forgets at its peril the principle that people are always more important than things.   *Matthew 6: 24*

PLEASURE

IF any man is wise, he will build his happiness on things which he cannot lose, things which are independent of the chances and the changes of this life. Robert Burns wrote of the fleeting things:

> *But pleasures are like poppies spread:*
> *You seize the flower, its bloom is shed;*
> *Or like the snow falls in the river,*
> *A moment white — then melts for ever.*

Any one whose happiness depends on things like that is doomed to disappointment. Any man whose treasure is in *things* is bound to lose his treasure, for in things there is no permanence, and no thing lasts forever.   *Matthew 6: 19-21*

IF everything which a man counts valuable is on this earth, then he will leave this earth reluctantly and grudgingly; if a man's thoughts have been ever in the world beyond, he will leave this world with gladness, because he goes at last to God.

Once Dr Samuel Johnson was shown through a noble castle and its grounds. When he had seen round it, he turned to his companions and said, 'These are the things which make it difficult to die'.

Jesus never said that this world was *un*important; but he said and implied over and over again that its importance is not in itself, but in that to which it leads. This world is not the end of life, it is a stage on the way; and therefore a man should never lose his heart to this world and to the things of this world. His eyes ought to be for ever fixed on the goal beyond.

Matthew 6: 22-23

PRAYER

GOD will never refuse our prayers; and God will never mock our prayers.

The Greeks had their stories about the gods who answered men's prayers, but the answer was an answer with a barb in it, a double-edged gift. Aurora, the goddess of the dawn, fell in love with Tithonus, a mortal youth – so the Greek story ran. Zeus, the king of the gods, offered her any gift that she might choose for her mortal lover. Aurora very naturally chose that Tithonus might live for ever; but she had forgotten to ask that Tithonus might remain for ever young; and so Tithonus grew older and older and older, and could never die, and the gift became a curse.

There is a lesson here: God will always answer our prayers; but *he will answer them in his way,* and his way will be the way of perfect wisdom and of perfect love.

Often, if he answered our prayers as we at the moment desired, it would be the worst thing possible for us, for in our ignorance we often ask for gifts which would be our ruin. This saying of Jesus tells us, not only that God will answer, but that God will answer in wisdom and in love.   *Matthew 7: 7-11*

PREJUDICE

I ONCE heard two theologians talking together. One was a younger man who was intensely interested in all that the new thinkers have to say; the other was an older man of a rigid and conventional orthodoxy.

The older man heard the younger man with a kind of half-contemptuous tolerance, and finally closed the conversation by saying, 'The old is better'.

Throughout all its history the Church has clung to the old. What Jesus is saying is that there comes a time when patching is folly, and when the only thing to do is to scrap something entirely and to begin again. There are forms of church government, there are forms of church service, there are forms of words expressing our beliefs, which we do often try to adjust and tinker with in order to bring them up to date; we try to patch them. No one would willingly, or recklessly, or callously abandon what has stood the test of time and of the years and in which former generations have found their comfort and put their trust; but the fact remains that this is a growing and an expanding universe: and there comes a time when patches are useless, and when a man and a church have to accept the adventure of the new, or withdraw into the backwater, where they worship, not God, but the past. *Matthew 9: 16-17*

PREJUDICE really means a *judging beforehand*. It is a judging before a man has examined the evidence, or a verdict given because of refusal to examine it. Few things have done more to hold things up than this. Nearly every forward step has had to fight against initial prejudice.

When Sir James Simpson discovered its use as an anaesthetic, especially in the case of childbirth, chloroform was held to be 'a decoy of Satan, apparently opening itself to bless women, but in the end hardening them, and robbing God of the deep, earnest cries, that should arise to him in time of trouble'. A prejudiced mind shuts out a man or woman from many a blessing.

Mark 5: 21-24

PRESTIGE

THERE is a story of Rabbi Tarphon. At the end of the fig harvest he was walking in a garden; and he ate some of the figs which had been left behind. The watchmen came upon him and beat him. He told them who he was, and because he was a famous Rabbi they let him go. All his life he regretted that he had used his status as a Rabbi to help himself.

'Yet all his days did he grieve, for he said, "Woe is me, for I have used the crown of the Law for my own profit"!'

Matthew 10: 8-10

PRIDE

THERE is a famous story of Roland, a knight at the court of Charlemagne, Holy Roman Emperor. He was in charge of the rearguard of the army and was suddenly caught by the Saracens at Roncesvalles. The battle raged fiercely against terrible odds.

Now Roland had a horn called Olivant which he had taken from the giant Jatmund, and its blast could be heard thirty miles away. So mighty was it that, so they said, the birds fell dead when its blast tore through the air.

Oliver, his friend, besought him to blow the horn so that Charlemagne would hear and come back to help. But Roland was too proud to ask for help. One by one his men fell fighting, till only he was left. Then at last, with his dying breath, he blew the horn, and Charlemagne came hasting back. But it was too late, for Roland was dead – because he was too proud to ask for help.

It is easy to think that we can handle life ourselves. But the way to find the miracles of the grace of God is to pocket our pride and humbly to confess our need and ask. Ask, and you will receive – but there is no receiving without asking.

Luke 8: 40-42; 49-56

QUAKERS

THERE have been two sets of people who completely refused all oaths.

There were the Essenes, an ancient sect of the Jews. Josephus, the Jewish historian of the first century AD, writes of them: 'They are eminent for fidelity and are ministers of peace. Whatsoever they say also is firmer than an oath. Swearing is avoided by them and they esteem it worse than perjury. For they say that he who cannot be believed without swearing is already condemned.'

There were, and still are, the Quakers. The Quakers will not, in any situation, submit to taking an oath. The utmost length to which George Fox would go was to use the word 'Verily'. He writes: 'I never wronged man or woman in all that time [the time that he worked in business]. While I was in that service, I used in my dealings the word *Verily*, and it was a common saying, "If George Fox says *Verily*, there is no altering him".'

In the ancient days, the Essenes would not in any circumstances take an oath, and to this day the Quakers are the same.

Matthew 5: 33-37

QUO VADIS?

THERE is a passage in the novel *Quo Vadis?* [*Where are You going?*] where Vinicius, the young Roman, has fallen in love with a girl who is a Christian. Because he is not a Christian, she will have nothing to do with him. He follows her to the secret night gathering of the little group of Christians, and there, unknown to anyone, he listens to the service. He hears Peter preach, and, as he listens, something happens to him:

'He felt that if he wished to follow that teaching, he would have to place on a burning pile all this thoughts, habits and character, his whole nature up to that moment, burn them into ashes and then fill himself with a life altogether different, and an entirely new soul.'

That *is* repentance. But what if a man has no other desire than to be left alone? The change is not necessarily from robbery, theft, murder, adultery and glaring sins. The change may be from a life that is completely selfish, instinctively demanding, totally inconsiderate, the change from a self-centred to a God-centred life – and a change like that hurts.

W M Macgregor quotes a saying of the Bishop in *Les Misérables:* 'I always bothered some of them; for through me the outside air came at them; my presence in their company made them feel as if a door had been left open and they were in a draught.'

Repentance is no sentimental feeling sorry; repentance is a revolutionary thing – that is why so few repent.

Mark 6: 12-13

REPENTANCE

DR John Hutton used to tell of a workman who had been a drunken reprobate and was converted. His workmates did their best to make him feel a fool. 'Surely,' they said to him, 'you can't believe in miracles and things like that. Surely, for instance, you don't believe that Jesus turned water into wine.'

'I don't know,' the man answered, 'whether he turned water into wine when he was in Palestine, but I do know that in my own house and home he has turned beer into furniture!'

There are any number of things in this world which we use every day without knowing how they work. Comparatively few of us know how electricity or radio or television works; but we do not deny that they exist because of that. Many of us drive a car with only the haziest notion of what goes on below its bonnet; but our lack of understanding does not prevent us using and enjoying the benefits which a car confers.

We may not understand how the Spirit works; but the effect of the Spirit on the lives of men is there for all to see. The unanswerable argument for Christianity is the Christian life. No man can disregard a faith which is able to make bad men good.

John 3: 7-13

REWARD

TO banish all rewards and punishments from the idea of religion is in effect to say that injustice has the last word. It cannot reasonably be held that the end of the good man and the end of the bad man are one and the same. That would simply mean that God does not care whether men are good or not. It would mean, to put it crudely and bluntly, that there is no point in being good, and no special reason why a man should live one kind of life instead of another. To eliminate all rewards and punishments is really to say that in God there is neither justice nor love.

Rewards and punishments are necessary in order to make sense of life. A E Housman, scholar and lyric poet, wrote:

Yonder, on the morning blink,
The sun is up, and so must I,
To wash and dress and eat and drink
And look at things and talk and think
And work, and God knows why.

And often have I washed and dressed,
And what's to show for all my pain?
Let me lie abed and rest:
Ten thousand times I've done my best,
And all's to do again.

If there are no rewards and no punishments, then that poem's view of life is true. Action is meaningless and all effort goes unavailingly whistling down the wind.   *Matthew 6: 1-18*

❖   ❖   ❖

WE cannot all be shining examples of goodness; we cannot all stand out in the world's eye as righteous; but he who helps a good man to be good receives a good man's reward.

H L Gee has a lovely story. There was a lad in a country village who, after a great struggle, reached the ministry. His helper in his days of study had been the village cobbler. The cobbler, like so many of his trade, was a man of wide reading and far thinking, and he had done much for the lad.

In due time the lad was licensed to preach. And on that day the cobbler said to him, 'It was always my desire to be a minister of the gospel, but the circumstances of my life made it impossible. But you are achieving what was closed to me. And I want you to promise me one thing – I want you to let me make and cobble your shoes – for nothing – and I want you to wear them in the pulpit when you preach, and then I'll feel you are preaching the gospel that I always wanted to preach standing in my shoes'.

Beyond a doubt the cobbler was serving God as the preacher was, and his reward would one day be the same.

Matthew 10: 40-43

RELIGION

INSTINCTIVELY people say, *'Don't disturb my religion'*. People say, 'Don't let unpleasant subjects disturb the pleasant decorum of my religion'.

Edmund Gosse points out a curious omission in the sermons of the famous divine, Jeremy Taylor: 'These sermons are amongst the most able and profound in the English language, but they hardly ever mention the poor, hardly ever refer to their sorrows, and show practically no interest in their state. The sermons were preached in South Wales where poverty abounded. The cry of the poor and the hungry, the ill-clothed and the needy, ceaselessly ascended up to heaven, and called out for pity and redress, but this eloquent divine never seemed to hear it; he lived and wrote and preached surrounded by the suffering and the needy, and yet remained scarcely conscious of their existence.'

It is much less disturbing to preach about the niceties of theological beliefs and doctrines than it is to preach about the needs of men and the abuses of life. We have actually known of congregations who informed ministers that it was a condition of their call that they would not preach on certain subjects. It was a notable thing that it was not what Jesus said about God that got him into trouble; it was what he said about *man* and about the needs of man that disturbed the orthodox of his day.

People have been known to say, 'Don't let personal relation-ships disturb my religion'.

James Burns quotes an amazing thing in this connection from the life of Angela di Foligras, the famous Italian mystic. She had the gift of completely withdrawing herself from this world, and of returning from her trances with tales of ineffably sweet communion with God. It was she herself who said: 'In that time, and by God's will, there died my mother, who was a great hindrance unto me in the following the way of God; my husband died likewise, and in a short time there died all my children. And because I had commenced to follow the aforesaid way, and had prayed God that he would rid me of them, I had great consolation of their deaths, albeit I did also feel some grief.' Her family was a trouble to her religion.

There is a type of religion which is fonder of committees than it is of housework; which is more set on quiet times than it is on human service. It prides itself on serving the Church and spending itself in devotion – but in God's eyes it has got things the wrong way round. *Mark 5: 14-17*

RICHES

IF everything a man desires is contained within this world, if all his interests are here, he never thinks of another world and of a hereafter. If a man has too big a stake on earth, he is very apt to forget that there is a heaven.

It is perfectly possible for a man to be so interested in earthly things that he forgets heavenly things; to be so involved in the things that are seen that he forgets the things that are unseen – and therein lies tragedy, for the things which are seen are temporal, but the things which are unseen are eternal.

Riches tend to make a man selfish. However much a man has, it is human for him to want still more, for, as it has been epigrammatically said, 'Enough is always a little more than a man has'. Further, once a man has possessed comfort and luxury, he always tends to fear the day when he may lose them. Life becomes a strenuous and worried struggle to retain the things he has. The result is that when a man becomes wealthy, instead of having the impulse to give things away, he very often has the impulse to cling on to them. His instinct is to amass more and more for the sake of the safety and the security which he thinks they will bring. The danger of riches is that they tend to make a man forget that he loses what he keeps, and gains what he gives away.

But Jesus did not say that it was *impossible* for a rich man to enter the Kingdom of Heaven. Zacchaeus was one of the richest men in Jericho, yet, all unexpectedly, he found the way in (Luke 19: 9). Joseph of Arimathaea was a rich man (Matthew 27: 57); Nicodemus must have been very wealthy, for he brought spices to anoint the dead body of Jesus, which were worth a king's ransom (John 19: 39).

It is not that those who have riches are shut out. It is not that riches are a sin — but they are a danger. The basis of all Christianity is an imperious sense of need; when a man has many things on earth, he is in danger of thinking that he does not need God; when a man has few things on earth, he is often driven to God because he has nowhere else to go.

Matthew 19: 23-26

ROADS

IN ancient times in the East the roads were bad. There was an eastern proverb which said: 'There are three states of misery — sickness, fasting and travel.' Before a traveller set out upon a journey, he was advised 'to pay all debts, provide for dependants, give parting gifts, return all articles under trust, take money and good-temper for the journey; then bid farewell to all'.

The ordinary roads were no better than tracks. They were not surfaced at all because the soil in Palestine is hard and will bear the traffic of mules and asses and oxen and carts. A journey along such a road was an adventure, and indeed an undertaking to be avoided.

There were some few surfaced and artificially made roads. Josephus, for instance, tells us that Solomon laid a causeway of black basalt stone along the roads that lead to Jerusalem to make them easier for pilgrims, and 'to manifest the grandeur of his riches and government'. All such surfaced and artificially made roads were originally built by the king and for the use of the king. They were called 'the king's highway'. They were kept in repair only as the king needed them for any journey that he might make. Before the king was due to arrive in any area, a message was sent to the people to get the king's roads in order for the king's journey.

Matthew 3: 1-6

SACRAMENT

A SACRAMENT is something, usually a very ordinary thing, which has acquired a meaning far beyond itself for him who has eyes to see and a heart to understand. There is nothing specially theological or mysterious about this.

In the house of everyone there is a drawer full of things which can only be called junk, and yet we will not throw them out, because when we touch and handle and look at them, they bring back this or that person, or this or that occasion. They are common things, but they have a meaning far beyond themselves. That is a sacrament.

When Sir James Barrie's mother died and they were clearing up her belongings, they found she had kept all the envelopes in which her famous son had posted her the cheques he so faithfully and lovingly sent. They were only old envelopes, but they meant much to her. That is a sacrament.

When Nelson was buried in St Paul's Cathedral, a party of his sailors bore this coffin to the tomb. One who saw the scene writes: 'With reverence and with efficiency they lowered the body of the world's greatest admiral into its tomb. Then, as though answering to a sharp order from the quarter-deck, they all seized the Union Jack with which the coffin had been covered and tore it to fragments, and each took his souvenir of the illustrious dead.'

All their lives that little bit of coloured cloth would speak to them of the admiral they had loved. That is a sacrament.

Luke 22: 7-23

SACRIFICE

IN the great Boulder Dam scheme in America, men lost their lives in that project which was to turn a dust-bowl into fertile land. When the scheme was completed, the names of those who had died were put on a tablet and the tablet was put into the great wall of the dam, and on it there was the inscription: 'These died that the desert might rejoice and blossom as the rose.'

The man who fights his battle for Christ will always make things easier for those who follow after. For them there will be one less struggle to be encountered on the way.

Matthew 5: 10-12

THE great men, whose names are on the honour roll of faith, well knew what they were doing.

After his trial in Scarborough Castle, the Quaker George Fox wrote: 'And the officers would often be threatening me, that I should be hanged over the wall ... they talked so much then of hanging me. But I told them, "If that was it they desired, and it was permitted them, I was *ready*".'

When John Bunyan was brought before the magistrate, he said: 'Sir, the law [the law of Christ] hath provided two ways of obeying: The one to do that which I in my conscience do believe that I am bound to do, actively; and where I cannot obey it actively, there I am willing to lie down and to suffer what they shall do unto me.'

The Christian may have to sacrifice his personal ambitions, the ease and the comfort that he might have enjoyed, the career that he might have achieved; he may have to lay aside his dreams, to realise that shining things of which he has caught a glimpse are not for him. He will certainly have to sacrifice his will, for no Christian can ever again do what he likes; he must do what Christ likes. In Christianity, there is always some cross — for it is the religion of the Cross.

Matthew 10: 34-39

SAFETY FIRST

A MAN has to choose sometimes between the closest ties of earth and loyalty to Jesus Christ.

John Bunyan knew all about that choice. The thing which

troubled him most about his imprisonment was the effect it would have upon his wife and children. What was to happen to them, bereft of his support?

'The parting with my wife and poor children hath often been to me in this place, as the pulling the flesh from my bones; and that not only because I am somewhat too fond of these great mercies, but also because I should have often brought to my mind the many hardships, miseries, and wants that my poor family was like to meet with, should I be taken from them, *especially my poor blind child*, who lay nearer my heart than all I had besides. O the thought of the hardship I thought my blind one might go under, would break up my heart to pieces .... But yet, recalling myself, thought I, I must venture you all with God, though it goeth to the quick to leave you; O I saw in this condition, I was a man who was pulling down his house upon the head of his wife and children; yet thought I, I must do it, I must do it.'

Once again, this terrible choice will come very seldom; in God's mercy to many of us it may never come; but the fact remains that all loyalties must give place to loyalty to God.

Matthew 10: 34-39

SHEPHERD

THE shepherd in Judaea had a hard and dangerous task. Pasture was scarce. The narrow central plateau was only a few miles wide, and then it plunged down to the wild cliffs and the terrible devastation of the desert. There were no restraining walls and the sheep could wander.

George Adam Smith wrote of the shepherd: 'On some high moor across which at night the hyaenas howl, when you meet him, sleepless, far-sighted, weather-beaten, armed, leaning on his staff and looking out over his scattered sheep, everyone of them on his heart, you understand why the shepherd of Judaea sprang to the front in his people's history; why they gave his name to the king and made him the symbol of providence; why Christ took him as the type of self-sacrifice.'

The shepherd was personally responsible for the sheep. If a sheep was lost, the shepherd must at least bring home the fleece to show how it had died. These shepherds were experts at tracking and could follow the straying sheep's footprints for miles across the hills. There was not a shepherd for whom it was not all in a day's work to risk his life for his sheep.

Many of the flocks were communal flocks, belonging not to individuals but to villages. There would be two or three shepherds in charge. Those whose flocks were safe would arrive home on time and bring news that one shepherd was still out on the mountain side searching for a sheep which was lost. The whole village would be upon the watch, and when, in the distance, they saw the shepherd striding home with the lost sheep across his shoulders, there would rise from the whole community a shout of joy and of thanksgiving.

That is the picture Jesus drew of God: that, said Jesus, is what God is like. God is as glad when a lost sinner is found, as a shepherd is when a strayed sheep is brought home. As a great saint said: 'God, too, knows the joy of finding things that have gone lost.'

There is a wondrous thought here. It is the truly tremendous truth that God is kinder than men. The orthodox would write off the tax-collector and the sinners as beyond the pale and as deserving of nothing but destruction; not so God. Men may give up hope of a sinner; not so God. God loves the folk who never stray away; but in his heart there is the joy of joys when a lost one is found and comes home. It is a thousand times easier to come back to God than to come home to the bleak criticism of men.

Souls of men! why will ye scatter
Like a crowd of frightened sheep?
Foolish hearts! why will ye wander
From a love so true and deep?

Was there ever kindest shepherd
Half so gentle, half so sweet,
As the Saviour who would have us
Come and gather round his feet?

For the love of God is broader
Than the measure of man's mind;
And the heart of the Eternal
Is most wonderfully kind.

Luke 15: 1-7

SIN

THERE is nothing in this world more terrible than to destroy someone's innocence. And, if a man has any conscience left, there is nothing which will haunt him more.

Someone tells of an old man who was dying; he was obviously sorely troubled. At last they got him to tell why. 'When we were boys at play,' he said, 'one day at a crossroads we reversed a signpost so that its arms were pointing the opposite way, and I've never ceased to wonder how many people were sent in the wrong direction by what we did.'

The sin of all sins is to teach another to sin.

Matthew 18: 5-7, 10

THE New Testament used five different words for sin.

The commonest word is *hamartia*. This was originally a shooting word and means *a missing of the target*. To fail to hit the target was *hamartia*. Therefore sin is *the failure to be what we might have been and could have been.*

Charles Lamb, the English essayist, has a picture of a man named Samuel le Grice. Le Grice was a brilliant youth who never fulfilled his promise. Lamb says that there were three stages in his career. There was a time when people said, 'He will do something'. There was a time when people said, 'He could do something if he would'. There was a time when people said, 'He might have done something, if he had liked'. Edwin Muir writes in his *Autobiography*: 'After a certain age all of us, good or bad, are grief stricken because of powers within us which have never been realised: because, in other words, we are not what we should be.

That precisely is *hamartia;* and that is precisely the situation in which we are all involved. Are we as good husbands or wives as we could be? Are we as good sons and daughters as we could be? Are we as good workmen or employers as we could be? Is there anyone who will dare to claim that he is all he might have been, and has done all he could have done? When we realise that sin means the failure to hit the target, the failure to be all that we might have been and could have been, then it is clear that every one of us is a sinner.

The second word for sin is *parabasis,* which literally means *a stepping across. Sin is the stepping across the line which is drawn between right and wrong.*

Do we always stay on the right side of the line which divides honesty and dishonesty in our lives?

Do we always stay on the right side of the lines which divides truth and falsehood? Do we never, by word or by silence, twist or evade or distort the truth?

Do we always stay on the right side of the line which divides kindness and courtesy from selfishness and harshness? Is there never an unkind action or a discourteous word in our lives?

When we think of it in this way, there can be none who can claim always to have remained on the right side of the dividing line.

The third word for sin is *paraptōma*, which means *a slipping across*. It is the kind of slip which a man might make on a slippery or icy road. It is not so deliberate as *parabasis*. Again and again we speak of words slipping out; again and again we are swept away by some impulse or passion, which has momentarily gained control of us, and which has made us lose our self-control. The best of us can slip into sin when for the moment we are off our guard.

The fourth word for sin is *anomia,* which means *lawlessness.* *Anomia* is the sin of the man who knows the right, and who yet does the wrong; the sin of the man who knows the law and who yet breaks the law. The first of all the human instincts is the instinct to do what we like; and therefore there comes into any man's life times when he wishes to kick over the traces and to defy the law, and to do or to take the forbidden thing. In *Mandalay,* Kipling makes the old soldier say:

> *Ship me somewheres east of Suez, where the best is like the worst.*
> *Where there ain't no Ten Commandments, an' a man can raise*
> *a thirst.*

Even if there are some who can say that they have never broken any of the Ten Commandments, there are none who can say that they have never wished to break any of them.

The fifth word for sin is the word *opheilēma* which is the word used in the body of the Lord's Prayer; and *opheilēma* means *a debt.* It means *a failure to pay that which is due,* a failure in duty. There can be no man who will ever dare to claim that he has perfectly fulfilled his duty to man and to God: such perfection does not exist among men.

So then, when we come to see what sin really is, we come to see that it is a universal disease in which every man is involved. Outward respectability in the sight of man, and inward sinfulness in the sight of God, may well go hand in hand. This, in fact, is a petition of the Lord's Prayer which every man needs to pray.

Matthew 6: 12,14,15

MANY a man would sin, if the only penalty he had to bear was the penalty he would have to bear himself; but he is saved from sin because he could not meet the pain that would appear in someone's eyes, if he made a shipwreck of his life.

Laura Richards has a parable like this:

A man sat by the door of his house smoking his pipe, and his neighbour sat beside him and tempted him. 'You are poor,' said the neighbour, 'and you are out of work and here is a way of bettering yourself. It will be an easy job and it will bring in money, and it is no more dishonest than things that are done every day by respectable people. You will be a fool to throw away such a chance as this. Come with me and we will settle the matter at once.' And the man listened. Just then his young wife came to the door of the cottage and she had her baby in her arms. 'Will you hold the baby for a minute,' she said. 'He is fretful and I must hang out the clothes to dry.' The man took the baby and held him on his knees. And as he held him, the child looked up, and the eyes of the child spoke: 'I am flesh of your flesh,' said the child's eyes. 'I am soul of your soul. Where you lead I shall follow. Lead the way, father. My feet after yours.' Then said the man to his neighbour: 'Go, and come here no more.'

A man might be perfectly willing to pay the price of sin, if that price affected only himself. But if he remembers that his sin will break someone else's heart, he will have a strong defence against temptation.   *Matthew 6: 13*

SON

A TRAVELLER tells how she was travelling in Georgia in the days before the Second World War. She was taken to see a very humble old woman in a little cottage. The old peasant woman asked her if she was going to Moscow. The traveller said she was. 'Then,' asked the woman, 'would you mind delivering a parcel of home-made toffee to my son? He cannot get anything like it in Moscow.' Her son's name was Josef Stalin. We do not normally think of the man who was once dictator of all the Russias as a man who liked toffee – but his mother did! For her the man-made labels did not matter.

Almost everybody would have regarded the woman in the crowd as totally unimportant. For Jesus she was someone in need, and therefore he, as it were, withdrew from the crowd and gave himself to her. 'God loves each one of us as if there was only one of us to love.'   *Luke 8: 43-48*

SLAVE

NO man can be a slave to two owners.

To understand all that this means and implies, we must remember two things about the slave in the ancient world. First, the slave in the eyes of the law was not a person but a thing. He had absolutely no rights of his own; his master could do with him absolutely as he liked. In the eyes of the law the slave was a *living tool*. His master could sell him, beat him, throw him out, and even kill him. His master possessed him as completely as he possessed any of his material possessions.

Second, in the ancient world a slave had literally no time which was his own. Every moment of his life belonged to his master. Under modern conditions a man has certain hours of work, and outside these hours of work his time is his own. It is indeed often possible for a man nowadays to find his real interest in life outside his hours of work. He may be a clerk in an office during the day and play the violin in an orchestra at night; and it may be that it is in his music that he finds his real life. He may work in a shipyard or in a factory during the day and run a youth club at night; and it may be that it is in the youth club that he find his real delight and the real expression of his personality. But it was far otherwise with the slave. The slave had literally no moment of time which belonged to himself. Every moment belonged to his owner and was at his owner's disposal.

Here, then, is our relationship to God. In regard to God we have no rights of our own; God must be undisputed master of our lives. We can never ask, 'What do I wish to do?' We must always ask, 'What does God wish me to do?' We have no time which is our own. We cannot sometimes say, 'I will do what God wishes me to do', and at other times say, 'I will do what I like'. The Christian has no time off from being a Christian; there is no time when he can relax his Christian standards, as if he was off duty. A partial or a spasmodic service of God is not enough. Being a Christian is a whole-time job. Nowhere in the Bible is the exclusive service which God demands more clearly set forth.

Jesus goes on to say, 'You cannot serve God and mamon.' The correct spelling is with one 'm'. *Mamon* was a Hebrew word for *material possessions*. Originally it was not a bad word at all. The Rabbis, for instance, had a saying, 'Let the *mamon* of thy neighbour be as dear to thee as thine own'. That is to say, a man should regard his neighbour's material possessions as being as sacrosanct as his own. But the word *mamon* has a most curious and a most revealing history. It comes from a root which means *to entrust;* and *mamon* was that which a man entrusted to a banker or to a safe deposit of some kind. *Mamon* was the wealth which a man entrusted to someone to keep safe for him.

But as the years went on, *mamon* came to mean not *that which is entrusted*, but *that in which a man put his trust*. The end of the process was that *mamon* came to be spelled with a capital 'M' and came to be regarded as nothing less than a god.

The history of that word shows vividly how material possessions can usurp a place in life which they were never meant to have. Originally a man's material possessions were the things which he entrusted to someone else for safekeeping; in the end they came to be the things in which a man puts his trust. Surely there is no better description of a man's god than to say that his god is the power in whom he trusts; and when a man puts his trust in material things, then material things have become, not his support, but his god.

Matthew 6: 24

SOW THE SEED

AN idea which may well change civilisation begins with one man.

In the British Empire it was William Wilberforce who was responsible for the freeing of the slaves. The idea of that liberation came to him when he read an exposure of the slave trade by Thomas Clarkson.

He was a close friend of William Pitt, then Prime Minister, and one day he was sitting with him and George Grenville in Pitt's garden at Holwood. It was a scene of beauty, with the Vale of Keston opening out before them, but the thoughts of Wilberforce were not on that but on the blots of the world. Suddenly Pitt turned to him: 'Wilberforce,' he said, 'why don't you give a notice of a motion on the slave-trade?'

An idea was sown in the mind of one man, and that idea changed life for hundreds of thousands of people. An idea must find a man willing to be possessed by it; but when it finds such a man, an unstoppable tide begins to flow.

Matthew 13: 31-32

ONE of the great stories of the Christian Church is the story of Telemachus. He was a hermit of the desert, but something told him – the call of God – that he must go to Rome. He went.

Rome was nominally Christian, but even in Christian Rome the gladiatorial games went on, in which men fought with each other, and crowds roared with the lust for blood. Telemachus found his way to the games. Eighty thousand people were there to spectate. He was horrified. Were these men slaughtering each other not also children of God? He leaped from his seat, right into the arena, and stood between the gladiators. He was tossed aside. He came back. The crowd were angry; they began to stone him. Still he struggled back between the gladiators. The prefect's command rang out; a sword flashed in the sunlight, and Telemachus was dead.

Suddenly there was a hush; suddenly the crowd realised what had happened – a holy man lay dead. Something happened that day to Rome, for there were never again any gladiatorial games. By his death one man had let loose something that cleansed an empire.

Someone must begin a reformation; he need not begin it in

a nation; he may begin it in his home or where he works. If he begins it no man knows where it will end.

Matthew 13: 31-32

SUFFERING

IN Carlisle Castle there is a little cell. Once long ago they put a Border chieftain in that cell and left him for years. In that cell there is one little window, which is placed too high for a man to look out of when he is standing on the floor. On the ledge of the window there are two depressions worn away in the stone. They are the marks of the hands of that Border chieftain, the place where, day after day, he lifted himself up by his hands to look out on the green dales across which he would never ride again.

Matthew 11: 1-6

BLESSED is the man who has endured the bitterest sorrow that life can bring.

The Arabs have a proverb: 'All sunshine makes a desert.' The land on which the sun always shines will soon become an arid place in which no fruit will grow. There are certain things which only the rains will produce; and certain experiences which only sorrow can beget.

Sorrow can do two things for us. It can show us, as nothing else can, the essential kindness of our fellow-men; and it can show us, as nothing else can, the comfort and the compassion of God. Many and many a man in the hour of his sorrow has discovered his fellow-men and his God as he never did before. When things go well it is possible to live for years on the surface of things; but when sorrow comes, a man is driven to the deep things of life; and, if he accepts it aright, a new strength and beauty enter into his soul.

I walked a mile with Pleasure,
She chattered all the way,
But left me none the wiser
For all she had to say.
I walked a mile with Sorrow,
And ne'er a word said she,
But, oh, the things I learned from her
When Sorrow walked with me!

Matthew 5: 4

SONS OF GOD

THERE are two kinds of sons. There is the son who never does anything else but use his home. All through his youth he takes everything that the home has to offer and gives nothing in return. His father may work and sacrifice to give him his chance in life, and he takes it as a right, never realising what he is taking and making no effort to deserve it or repay it. When he leaves home, he makes no attempt to keep in touch. The home has served his purpose and he is finished with it. He realises no bond to be maintained and no debt to be paid. He is his father's son; to his father he owes his existence; and to his father he owes what he is; but between him and his father there is no bond of love and intimacy. The father has given all in love; but the son has given nothing in return.

On the other hand, there is the son who all his life realises what his father is doing and has done for him. He takes every opportunity to show his gratitude by trying to be the son his father would wish him to be; as the years go on he grows closer and closer to his father; the relationship of father and son becomes the relationship of fellowship and friendship. Even when he leaves home the bond is still there, and he is still conscious of a debt that can never be repaid.

In the one case the son grows further and further away from the father; in the other he grows nearer and nearer the father.

Both are sons, but the sonship is very different. The second has become a son in a way that the first never was.

We may illustrate this kind of relationship from another, but a kindred, sphere. The name of a certain younger man was mentioned to a famous teacher, whose student the young man claimed to be. The older man answered: 'He may have attended my lectures, but he was not one of my students.' There is a world of difference between sitting in a teacher's class room and being one of his students. There can be contact without communication; there can be relationship without fellowship.

All men are the sons of God in the sense that they owe to him the creation and the preservation of their lives; but only some men become the sons of God in the depth and intimacy of the true father and son relationship.

John 1: 12-13

TEMPTATION

IT is through our inmost thoughts and desires that the tempter comes to us. His attack is launched in our own minds. It is true that that attack can be so real that we almost see the devil. To this day you can see the ink-stain on the wall of Luther's room in the Castle of Wartburg in Germany; Luther caused that ink-stain by throwing his ink-pot at the devil as he tempted him. But the very power of the devil lies in the fact that he breaches our defences and attacks us from within. He find his allies and his weapons in our own inmost thoughts and desires.

Matthew 4: 1-11

PLATO likened the soul to a charioteer whose task it was to drive two horses. The one horse was gentle and biddable and obedient to the reins and to the word of command; the other horse was wild and untamed and rebellious. The name of the one horse was reason; the name of the other was passion.

Life is always a conflict between the demands of the passions and the control of the reason. The reason is the leash which keeps the passions in check. But, *a leash may snap at any time.* Self-control may be for a moment off its guard – and then what may happen? So long as there is this inner tension, this inner conflict, life must be insecure. In such circumstances there can be no such thing as safety. The only way to safety, Jesus said, is to eradicate the desire for the forbidden thing for ever. Then, and then alone, life is safe.

Matthew 5: 21-48

SOMETIMES the attack of temptation comes from outside us. There are people whose influence is bad. There are people in whose company it would be very difficult even to suggest doing a dishonourable thing, and there are people in whose company it is easy to do the wrong thing.

When Robert Burns was a young man, he went to Irvine to learn flax-dressing. There he fell in with a certain Robert Brown, who was a man who had seen much of the world, and who had a fascinating and a dominating personality. Burns tells us that he admired him and strove to imitate him. Burns goes on: 'He was the only man I ever saw who was a greater fool than myself when Woman was the guiding star .... He spoke of a certain fashionable failing with levity, which hitherto I had regarded with horror .... Here his friendship did me a mischief.'

There are friendships and associations which can do us a mischief. In a tempting world, a man should be very careful in his choice of friends and of the society in which he will move. He should give the temptations which come from outside as little chance as possible. *Matthew 6: 13*

TOLERANCE

WE have a tendency to brand as a heretic anyone who does not think as we do.

John Wesley, founder of Methodism, was the greatest example of tolerance in the world. 'We think,' he said, 'and we let think.'

'I have no more right,' he said, 'to object to a man for holding a different opinion from mine than I have to differ with a man because he wears a wig and I wear my own hair.'

Wesley had one greeting: 'Is thy heart as my heart? Then give me thy hand!'

It is good for a man to have the assurance that he is right, but that is no reason why he should have the conviction that everyone else is wrong. *Mark 4: 30-32*

❖ ❖ ❖

THERE is far more than one way to God. 'God,' as Tennyson has it, 'fulfils himself in many ways.' The Spanish novelist and dramatist Cervantes once said, 'Many are the roads by which God carries his own to heaven'. The world is round, and two people can get to precisely the same destination by starting out in precisely opposite directions. All roads, if we pursue them long enough and far enough, lead to God. It is a fearful thing for any man or any Church to think that he or it has a monopoly of salvation.

It is necessary to remember that truth is always bigger than any man's grasp of it. No man can possibly grasp all truth. The basis of tolerance is not a lazy acceptance of anything. It is not the feeling that there cannot be assurance anywhere. The basis of tolerance is simply the realisation of the magnitude of the orb of truth. John Morley wrote: 'Toleration means reverence for all the possibilities of truth, it means acknowledgement that she dwells in divers mansions, and wears vesture of many colours, and speaks in strange tongues. It means frank respect for freedom of indwelling conscience against mechanical forms, official conventions, social force. It means the charity that is greater than faith or hope.' Intolerance is a sign both of arrogance and ignorance, for it is a sign that a man believes that there is no truth beyond the truth he sees.

Not only must we concede to every man the right to do his own thinking, we must also concede the right to a man to do his own speaking. Of all democratic rights the dearest is that of liberty of speech. There are, of course, limitations. If a man is inculcating doctrines calculated to destroy morality and to remove the foundations from all civilised and Christian society, he must be combatted. But the way to combat him is certainly not to eliminate him by force, but to prove him wrong. Once Voltaire, the French philosopher and writer, laid down the conception of freedom of speech in a vivid sentence: 'I hate what you say,' he said, 'but I would die for your right to say it.'

We must remember that any doctrine or belief must finally be judged by the kind of people it produces. Dr Thomas Chalmers, the eminent theologian, once put the matter in a nutshell: 'Who cares,' he demanded, 'about any Church but as an instrument of Christian good?' The question must always ultimately be not 'How is a Church governed?', but 'What kind of people does a Church produce?' *Mark 9: 38-40*

❖ ❖ ❖

THERE is an old eastern fable. A man possessed a ring set with a wonderful opal. Whoever wore the ring became so sweet and true in character than all men loved him. The ring was a charm. Always it was passed down from father to son, and always it did its work.

As time went on, it came to a father who had three sons who he loved with an equal love. What was he to do when the time came to pass on the ring? The father got another two rings made precisely the same so that none could tell the difference. On his death-bed he called each of his sons in, spoke the same words of love, and to each, without telling the others, gave a ring.

When the three sons discovered that each had a ring, a great dispute arose as to which was the true ring that could do so much for its owner. The case was taken to a wise judge. He examined the rings and then he spoke: 'I cannot tell which is the magic ring,' he said, 'but you yourselves can prove it.' 'We?' asked the sons in astonishment. 'Yes,' said the judge, 'for if the true ring gives sweetness to the character of the man who wears it, then I and all the other people in the city will know the man who possesses the true ring by the goodness of his life. So, go your ways, and be kind, be truthful, be brave, be just in your dealings, and he who does these things will be the owner of the true ring.'

The matter was to be proved by life. No man can entirely condemn beliefs which make a man good. If we remember that, we may be less intolerant.

We may hate a man's beliefs, but we must never hate the man. We may wish to eliminate what he teaches, but we must never wish to eliminate him.

He drew a circle that shut me out –
Rebel, heretic, thing to flout.
But love and I had the wit to win –
We drew a circle that took him in.

Mark 9: 38-40

TRADITION

NO man can lightly fail the traditions and heritage into which he has entered, and which have taken generations to build up.

When Pericles, the greatest of the statesmen of Athens, was going to address the Athenian Assembly, he always whispered to himself: 'Pericles, remember that you are an Athenian and that you go to speak to Athenians.'

One of the epics of the Second World War was the defence of Tobruk. The Coldstream Guards cut their way out of Tobruk, but only a handful of them survived, and even these were just shadows of men. Two hundred survivors out of two battalions were being cared for by the RAF. A Coldstream Guards officer was in the mess. Another officer said to him, 'After all, as Foot Guards, you have no option but to have a go'. And an RAF man standing there said, 'It must be pretty tough to be in the Brigade of Guards, because tradition compels you to carry on irrespective of circumstances'.

The power of a tradition is one of the greatest things in life. We belong to a country, a school, a family, a Church. What we do affects that to which we belong. We cannot lightly betray the traditions into which we have entered.   *Matthew 6: 13*

TREASURE

BOTH Jesus and the Jewish Rabbis were sure that what is selfishly hoarded is lost, but what is generously given away brings treasure in heaven.

That was also the principle of the Christian Church in the days to come. The Early Church always lovingly cared for the poor, and the sick, and the distressed, and the helpless, and those for whom no one else cared.

In the days of the terrible Decian persecution in Rome, the Roman authorities broke into a Christian Church. They were out to loot the treasures which they believed the Church to possess. The Roman prefect demanded from Laurentius, the deacon: 'Show me your treasures at once.' Laurentius pointed at the widows and orphans who were being fed, the sick who were being nursed, the poor whose needs were being supplied. 'These,' he said, 'are the treasures of the Church.'

The Church has always believed that 'what we keep, we lose; and what we spend, we have'. *Matthew 6: 19-21*

TRUTH

IT is always dangerous to speak the truth; and yet although the man who allies himself with the truth may end in gaol or on the scaffold, in the final count he is the victor.

Once the Earl of Morton, who was regent of Scotland, threatened Andrew Melville, the reformer. 'There will never,' he said menacingly, 'be quietness in this country till half a dozen of you be hanged or banished.' Melville answered him, 'Tush! sir, threaten not your courtiers in that fashion. It is the same to me whether I rot in the air or in the ground .... God be glorified, it will not lie in your power to hang nor exile his truth'.

Plato once said that the wise man will always choose to suffer wrong rather than to do wrong. We need only ask ourselves whether in the last analysis and at the final assize we would prefer to be Herod Antipas or John the Baptist.

Luke 3: 19-20

ONE of the old missionaries came to one of the ancient Pictish kings. The king asked him what he might expect if he became a Christian. The missionary answered: 'You will find wonder upon wonder and every one of them true.'

Sometimes when we travel a very lovely road, vista after vista opens to us. At every view we think that nothing could be lovelier, and then we turn another corner and an even greater loveliness opens before us. When a man enters on the study of some great subject, like music or poetry or art, he never gets to the end of it. Always there are fresh experiences of beauty waiting for him.

It is so with Christ. The more we know of him, the more wonderful he becomes. The longer we live with him, the more loveliness we discover. The more we think about him and with him, *the wider the horizon of truth becomes.*

This phrase may be John's way of expressing the limitlessness of Christ. It may be his way of saying that the man who companies with Christ will find new wonders dawning upon his soul and enlightening his mind and enchaining his heart every day.

John 1: 15-17

❖   ❖   ❖

THERE are certain truths which a man cannot *accept;* he must *discover* them for himself.

Just as Nicodemus did, the woman took the words of Jesus quite literally when she was meant to understand them spiritually. It was *living* water of which Jesus spoke. In ordinary language, to the Jew *living* water was *running* water. It was the water of the running stream in contradistinction to the water of the stagnant cistern or pool. This well, as we have seen, was not a springing well, but a well into which the water percolated from the subsoil. To the Jew, *running, living* water from the stream was always better. So the woman is saying: 'You are offering me pure stream water. Where are you going to get it?'

She goes on to speak of 'our father Jacob'. The Jews would, of course, have strenuously denied that Jacob was the father of the Samaritans, but it was part of the Samaritan claim that they were descended from Joseph, the son of Jacob, by way of Ephraim and Manasseh. The woman is in effect saying to Jesus: 'This is blasphemous talk. Jacob, our great ancestor, when he came here, had to dig this well to gain water for his family and his cattle. Are you claiming to be able to get fresh, running stream water? If you are, you are claiming to be wiser and more powerful than Jacob. That is a claim that no one has any right to make.'

When people were on a journey they usually carried with them a bucket made from the skin of some beast so that they could draw water from any well at which they halted. No doubt Jesus' band had such a bucket; and no doubt the disciples had taken it into the town with them. The woman saw that Jesus did not possess such a traveller's leathern bucket, and so again she says in effect: 'You need not talk about drawing water and giving it to me. I can see for myself that you have not a bucket with which to draw water.'

H B Tristram begins his book, entitled *Eastern Customs in Bible Lands,* with this personal experience. He was sitting beside a well in Palestine, beside the scene of the inn which figures in the story of the Good Samaritan:

> *An Arab woman came down from the hills above to draw water; she unfolded and opened her goatskin bottle, and then untwined a cord, and attached it to a very small leathern bucket which she carried, by means of which she slowly filled her skin, fastened its mouth, placed it on her shoulder, and, bucket in hand, climbed the mountain. I thought of the woman of Samaria at Jacob's well, when an Arab footman, toiling up the steep path from Jericho, heated and wearied with his journey, turned aside to the well, knelt and peered wistfully down. But he had 'nothing to draw with and the well was deep'. He lapped a little moisture from the water spilt by the woman who had preceded him, and, disappointed, passed on. It was just that that the woman was thinking of when she said that Jesus had nothing wherewith to draw water from the depths of the well.*

> *John 4: 10-15*

THE UNFORGIVEN

TO sin is terrible, but to teach another to sin is infinitely worse.

O. Henry, the American short-story writer, has a story in which he tells of a little girl whose mother was dead. Her father used to come home from work and sit down and take off his jacket and open his paper and light his pipe and put his feet on the mantelpiece. The little girl would come in and ask him to play with her for a little for she was lonely. He told her he was tired, to let him be at peace. He told her to go out to the street and play. She played on the streets. The inevitable happened – she took to the streets.

The years passed on and she died. Her soul arrived in heaven. Peter saw her and said to Jesus, 'Master, here's a girl who was a bad lot. I suppose we send her straight to hell?' 'No,' said Jesus gently, 'let her in. Let her in.' And then his eyes grew stern. 'But look for a man who refused to play with his little girl and sent her out to the streets – *and send him to hell.*' God is not hard on the sinner, but he will be stern to the person who makes it easier for another to sin, and whose conduct, either thoughtless or deliberate, puts a stumbling-block in the path of a weaker brother.   *Mark 9: 41-42*

USELESSNESS

SO then there are three ways in which we can be useless branches. We can refuse to listen to Jesus Christ at all. We can listen to him, and then render him a lip service unsupported by any deeds. We can accept him as Master, and then, in face of the difficulties of the way or the desire to do as we like, abandon him. One thing we must remember. It is a first principle of the New Testament that *uselessness invites disaster.* The fruitless branch is on the way to destruction.   *John 15: 1-10*

VISION

JESUS can open our eyes until we are able to see the truth.

In one of William J Locke's novels, there is a picture of a woman who has any amount of money, and who has spent half a life time on a tour of the sights and picture galleries of the world. She is weary and bored. Then she meets a Frenchman who has little of this world's goods, but who has a wide knowledge and a great love of beauty. He comes with her, and in his company things are completely different. 'I never knew what things were like,' she said to him, 'until you taught me how to look at them.'

Life is quite different when Jesus teaches us how to look at things. When Jesus comes into our hearts, he opens our eyes to see things truly. *Matthew 1: 18-25*

VALUES

A MAN may gain his possessions at the expense of honesty and honour.
George Macdonald tells of a village shopkeeper who grew very rich. Whenever he was measuring cloth, he measured it with his two thumbs inside the measure, so that he always gave short measure. George Macdonald says of him: 'He took from his soul, and he put it in his siller-bag.' A man can enrich his bank account at the expense of impoverishing his soul.

A man may gain his possessions by deliberately smashing some weaker rival. Many a man's success is founded on someone else's failure. Many a man's advancement has been gained by pushing someone else out of the way. It is hard to see how a man who prospers in such a way can sleep at nights.

A man may gain his possessions at the expense of still higher duties. Robertson Nicoll, the great editor, was born in a manse in the north-east of Scotland. His father had one passion: to buy and to read books. He was a minister and he never had more than £200 a year. But he amassed the greatest private library in Scotland amounting to 17,000 books. He did not use them in his sermons; he was simply consumed to own and to read them. When he was forty he married a girl of 24. In eight years she was dead of tuberculosis; of a family of five, only two lived to be over twenty. That cancerous growth of books filled every room and every passage of the manse. It may have delighted the owner of the books, but it killed his wife and family.   *Matthew 6: 24*

❖   ❖   ❖

WHEN Jesus came to Nazareth, he put himself to a very severe test. He was coming to his home town; and there are no severer critics of any man than those who have known him since his boyhood. It was never meant to be a private visit simply to see his old home and his own people. He came attended by his disciples. That is to say, he came as a Rabbi. The Rabbis moved about the country accompanied by their little circle of disciples, and it was as a teacher, with his disciples, that Jesus came.

He went into the synagogue and he taught. His teaching was greeted not with wonder, but with a kind of contempt. 'They took offence at him.' They were scandalised that a man who came from a background like Jesus should say and do things such as he. Familiarity had bred a mistaken contempt.

They refused to listen to what he had to say for two reasons.

They said, 'Is not this the carpenter?' The word used for carpenter is *tektōn*. Now *tektōn* does mean a worker in wood, but it means more than merely a joiner. It means a *craftsman*. In Homer the *tektōn* is said to build ships and houses and temples. In the old days, and still today in many places, there could be found in little towns and villages a craftsman who would build you anything from a chicken-coop to a house; the kind of man who could build a wall, mend a roof, repair a gate; the craftsman, the handy-man, who, with few or no instruments and with the simplest tools, could turn his hand to any job. That is what Jesus was like. But the point is that the people of Nazareth despised Jesus *because he was a working man*. He was a man of the people, a layman, a simple man – and therefore they despised him.

One of the leaders of the Labour movement was that great soul Will Crooks. He was born into a home where one of his earliest recollections was seeing his mother crying because she had no idea where the next meal was to come from. He started work in a blacksmith's shop at five shillings a week. He became a fine craftsman and one of the bravest and straightest men who ever lived. He entered municipal politics and became the first Labour Mayor of a London borough.

There were people who were offended when Will Crooks became Mayor of Poplar. In a crowd one day, a lady said with great disgust, 'They've made that common fellow Crooks mayor, and he's no better than a working man'. A man in the crowd – Will Crooks himself – turned round and raised his hat: 'Quite right, madam,' he said. 'I am not better than a working man.'

The people of Nazareth despised Jesus because he was a working man. To us that is his glory, because it means that God, when he came to earth, claimed no exemptions. He took upon himself the common life with all its common tasks.

The accidents of birth, fortune and pedigree have nothing to do with manhood. Pope, the English poet and satirist, wrote:

Worth makes the man, and want of it the fellow;
The rest is all but leather or prunello.

As Burns had it:

A prince can mak' a belted knight,
A marquis, duke, an' a' that!
But an honest man's aboon his might –
Guid faith, he mauna fa' that!
For a' that, an' a' that,
The pith o' sense an' pride o' worth
Are higher rank than a' that.

We must ever beware of the temptation to evaluate men by externals and incidentals, and not by native worth.

Mark 6: 1-6

❖   ❖   ❖

A J CRONIN tells of a district nurse he knew when he was in practice as a doctor. For twenty years, single-handed, she had served a ten-mile district. 'I marvelled,' he says, 'at her patience, her fortitude and her cheerfulness. She was never too tired at night to rise for an urgent call. Her salary was most inadequate, and late one night, after a particularly strenuous day, I ventured to protest to her, "Nurse, why don't you make them pay you more? God knows you are worth it". "If God knows I'm worth it," she answered, "that's all that matters to me".'

She was working, not for men, but for God. And when we work for God, prestige will be the last thing that enters into our mind, for we will know that even our best is not good enough for him.   *Luke 9: 46-48*

THE WAY

JOHN Oxenham wrote:

To every man there openeth
A way and ways and a way;
And the high soul treads the high way.
And the low soup gropes the low;
And in between on the misty flats
The rest drift to and fro;
But to every man there openeth
A high way and a low;
And every man decideth
The way his soul shall go.

THAT is the choice with which Jesus is confronting men in this passage. There is a broad and an easy way, and there are many who take it; but the end of it is ruin. There is a narrow and a hard way, and there are few who take it; but the end of it is life.

Cebes, the disciple of Socrates, writes in the *Tabula:* 'Dost thou see a little door, and a way in front of the door, which is not much crowded, but the travellers are few? That is the way that leadeth to true instruction.'   *Matthew 7: 13-14*

THERE is never any easy way to greatness; greatness is always the product of toil.

Hesiod, the old Greek poet, writes: 'Wickedness can be had in abundance easily; smooth is the road, and very nigh she dwells; but in front of virtue the gods immortal have put sweat.'

Epicharmus said: 'The gods demand of us toil as the price of all good things' .... 'Knave,' he warns, 'yearn not for the soft things, lest thou earn the hard.'

Once Edmund Burke, the eighteenth century political and philosophical writer, made a great speech in the House of Commons. Afterwards his brother, Richard Burke, was observed deep in thought. He was asked what he was thinking about, and answered: 'I have been wondering how it has come about that Ned has contrived to monopolise all the talents of our family; but then again I remember that, when we were at play, he was always at work.'

Even when a thing is done with an appearance of ease, that ease is the product of unremitting toil. The skill of the master executant on the piano, or the champion player on the golf course, did not come without sweat. There never has been any other way to greatness than the way of toil, and anything else which promises such a way is a delusion and a snare.

Matthew 7: 13-14

JESUS says, 'Woe to you who are rich because you have all the comfort you are going to get'. The word Jesus uses for *have* is the word used for receiving payment in full of an account. What Jesus is saying is this: 'If you set your heart and bend your whole energies to obtain the things which the world values, you will get them – but that is *all* you will ever get.' In the expressive modern phrase, literally, you have had it!

But if, on the other hand, you set your heart and bend all your energies to be utterly loyal to God and true to Christ, you will run into all kinds of trouble; you may by the world's standards look unhappy, but much of your payment is still to come; and it will be joy eternal.

We are here face to face with an eternal choice which begins in childhood and never ends till life ends. Will you take the easy way which yields immediate pleasure and profit? Or will you take the hard way which yields immediate toil and sometimes suffering? Will you seize on the pleasure and the profit of the moment? Or will you concentrate on Christ? If you take the world's way, you must abandon the values of Christ. If you take Christ's way, you must abandon the values of the world.

Jesus had no doubt which way in the end brought happiness. F R Maltby said: 'Jesus promised his disciples three things – that they would be completely fearless, absurdly happy, and in constant trouble.' G K Chesterton, whose principles constantly got him into trouble, once said, 'I like getting into hot water. It keeps you clean!' It is Jesus' teaching that the joy of heaven will amply compensate for the trouble of earth. As Paul said, 'This slight momentary affliction is preparing for us an eternal weight of glory beyond all comparison' (2 Corinthians 4:17). The challenge of the Beatitudes is: 'Will you be happy in the world's way, or in Christ's way?'

Luke 6: 20-26

THE WILL OF GOD

THE most important thing in the world is to obey the will of God; the most important words in the world are 'Thy will be done'. But it is equally clear that the frame of mind and the tone of voice in which these words are spoken will make a world of difference.

A man may say 'Thy will be done' in a tone of defeated resignation. He may say it, not because he wishes to say it, but because he has accepted the fact that he cannot possibly say anything else. He may say it because he has accepted the fact that God is too strong for him, and that it is useless to batter his head against the walls of the universe. He may say it thinking only of the ineluctable power of God which has him in its grip. As Omar Khayyam had it:

> *But helpless Pieces of the Game He plays*
> *Upon this Chequer-board of Nights and Days;*
> *Hither and thither moves, and checks, and slays,*
> *And one by one back in the closet lays.*

> *The Ball no question makes of Ayes and Noes,*
> *But Here and There as strikes the Player goes;*
> *And He that Toss'd you down into the Field,*
> *He knows about it all — He knows — HE knows!*

A man may accept the will of God for no other reason than that he has realised that he cannot do anything else.

A man may say 'Thy will be done' in a tone of bitter resentment. Swinburne spoke of men feeling the trampling of the iron feet of God. He speaks of the supreme evil, God. Beethoven died all alone; and it is said that when they found his body, his lips were drawn back in a snarl and his fists were clenched as if he were shaking his fists in the very face of God and of high heaven. A man may feel God is his enemy, and yet an enemy so strong that he cannot resist. He may therefore accept God's will, but he may accept it with bitter resentment and smouldering anger.

A man may say 'Thy will be done' in perfect love and trust. He may say it gladly and willingly, no matter what that will may be. It should be easy for the Christian to say 'Thy will be done' like that; for the Christian can be very sure of two things about God.

He can be sure of the *wisdom* of God. Sometimes when we want something built or constructed, or altered or repaired, we take it to the craftsman and consult him about it. He makes some suggestion, and we often end up by saying: 'Well, do what you think best. You are the expert.' God is the expert in life, and his guidance can never lead anyone astray.

When Richard Cameron, the Scottish Covenanter, was killed, his head and his hands were cut off by one Murray and taken to Edinburgh. 'His father being in prison for the same cause, the enemy carried them to him, to add grief unto his former sorrow, and inquired at him if he knew them. Taking his son's head and hands, which were very fair (being a man of fair complexion like himself), he kissed them and said, "I know them – I know them. They are my son's – my own dear son's. It is the Lord. Good is the will of the Lord, who cannot wrong me or mine, but hath made goodness and mercy to follow us all our days".'

When a man can speak like that, when he is quite sure that his times are in the hands of the infinite wisdom of God, it is easy to say 'Thy will be done'.

He can be sure of the *love* of God. We do not believe in a mocking and a capricious God, or in a blind and iron determinism. Thomas Hardy finishes his novel *Tess of the d'Urbervilles* with the grim words: 'The President of the Immortals had ended his sport with Tess.' We believe in a God whose name is love. As Whittier had it:

> *I know not where His islands lift*
> *Their fronded palms in air.*
> *I only know I cannot drift*
> *Beyond His love and care.*

As Browning triumphantly declared his faith:

> *God, Thou art love! I build my faith on that ...*
> *I know thee who has kept my path and made*
> *Light for me in the darkness, tempering sorrow*
> *So that it reached me like a solemn joy.*
> *It were too strange that I should doubt thy love.*

And as Paul had it: 'He who did not spare his own Son, but gave him up for us all, will he not also give us all things with him?' (Romans 8: 32).

No man can look at the Cross and doubt the love of God, and when we are sure of the love of God, it is easy to say – 'Thy will be done'. *Matthew 6: 10*

THIS WORLD

THERE is a story of a conversation between a young and ambitious lad and an older man who knew life.

Said the young man, 'I will learn my trade.'

'And then?' said the older man.

'I will set up in business.'

'And then?'

'I will make my fortune.'

'And then?'

'I suppose that I shall grow old and retire and live on my money.'

'And then?'

'Well, I suppose that some day I will die.'

'And then?' came the last stabbing question.

The man who never remembers that there is another world is destined some day for the grimmest of grim shocks.

Luke 12: 13-14

IN the days of persecution a certain danger always threatened the Christian witness. There always were those who actually courted martyrdom; they were wrought up to such a pitch of hysterical and fanatical enthusiasm that they went out of their way to become martyrs for the faith.

Jesus was wise. He told his men that there must be no wanton waste of Christian lives; that they must not pointlessly and needlessly throw their lives away. As some one has put it, the life of every Christian witness is precious, and must not be recklessly thrown away. 'Bravado is not martyrdom.' Often the Christians had to die for their faith, but they must not throw away their lives in a way that did not really help the faith. As it was later said, a man must contend *lawfully* for the faith.

When Jesus spoke like this, he was speaking in a way which Jews would recognise and understand. No people were ever more persecuted than the Jews have always been; and no people were ever clearer as to where the duties of the martyr lay. The teaching of the great Rabbis was quite clear. When it was a question of *public sanctification* or *open profanation* of God's name, duty was plain – a man must be prepared to lay down his life. But when that public declaration was not in question, a man might save his life by breaking the law; but for no reason must he commit idolatry, unchastity, or murder.

The case the Rabbis cited was this: suppose a Jew is seized by a Roman soldier, and the soldier says mockingly, and with no other intention than to humiliate and to make a fool of the Jew, 'eat this pork', then the Jew may eat, for 'God's laws are given for life and not for death'. But suppose the Roman says: 'Eat this pork as a sign that you renounce Judaism: eat this pork as a sign that you are ready to worship Jupiter and the Emperor' – the Jew must die rather than eat. In any time of official persecution, the Jew must die rather than abandon his faith. As the Rabbis said: 'The words of the Law are only firm in that man who would die for their sake.'

The Jew was forbidden to throw his life in a needless act of pointless martyrdom; but when it came to a question of true witness, he must be prepared to die. *Matthew 10: 23*

XENOPHON

THE Greeks used to tell how Xenophon, the Athenian historian and philosopher of the fifth century BC, first met Socrates. Socrates met him in a narrow lane and barred his path with his stick. First of all Socrates asked him if he knew where he could buy this and that, and if he knew where this and that were made. Xenophon gave the required information. The Socrates asked him, 'Do you know where men are made good and virtuous?'

'No,' said the young Xenophon.

'Then,' said Socrates, 'follow me and learn!'

Jesus, too, called on these fishermen to follow him. It is interesting to note what kind of men they were. They were not men of great scholarship, or influence, or wealth, or social background. They were not poor, they were simple working people with no great background, and certainly, anyone would have said, with no great future. It was these ordinary men whom Jesus chose.

Once there came to Socrates a very ordinary man called Aeschines. 'I am a poor man,' said Aeschines. 'I have nothing else, but I give you myself.'

'Do you not see,' said Socrates, 'that you are giving me the most precious thing of all?'

What Jesus needs is ordinary folk who will give him themselves. He can do anything with people like that.

Matthew 4: 18-22

YOKE

JESUS invites us to take his yoke upon our shoulders. The Jews used the phrase *the yoke* for entering *into submission to*. They spoke of the yoke of the Law, the yoke of the commandments, the yoke of the Kingdom, the yoke of God. But it may well be that Jesus took the words of his invitation from something much nearer home that that.

He says: 'My yoke is *easy*.' The word *easy* is in Greek *chrēstos,* which can mean *well-fitting*. In Palestine ox-yokes were made of wood. The ox was brought, and the measurements were taken. The yoke was then roughed out, and the ox was brought back to have the yoke tried on. The yoke was carefully adjusted, so that it would fit well, and not gall the neck of the patient beast. The yoke was tailor-made to fit the ox.

There is a legend that Jesus made the best ox-yokes in all Galilee, and that from all over the country men came to him to buy the best yokes that skill could make. In those days, as now, shops had their signs above the door; and it has been suggested that the sign above the door of the carpenter's shop in Nazareth may well have been: 'My yokes fit well.' It may well be that Jesus is here using a picture from the carpenter's shop in Nazareth where he had worked throughout the silent years.

Jesus says: 'My yoke fits well.' What he means is: 'The life I give you is not a burden to gall you; your task is made to measure to fit you.' Whatever God sends us is made to fit our needs and our abilities exactly.

Jesus says: 'My burden is light.' As a Rabbi had it: 'My burden is become my song.' It is not that the burden is easy to carry; but it is laid on us in love; it is meant to be carried in love; and love makes even the heaviest burden light. When we remember the love of God, when we know that our burden is to love God and to love men, then the burden becomes a song.

There is an old story which tells how a man came upon a little boy carrying a still smaller boy, who was lame, upon his back. 'That's a heavy burden for you to carry,' said the man. 'That's no' a burden,' came the answer. 'That's my wee brother.'

The burden which is given in love and carried in love is always light. *Matthew 11: 28-30*

ZACCHAEUS

ZACCHAEUS took steps to show all the community that he was a changed man. When Jesus announced that he would stay that day at his house, and when he discovered that he had found a new and wonderful friend, immediately Zacchaeus took a decision. He decided to give half of his goods to the poor; the other half he did not intend to keep to himself, but to use to make restitution for the frauds of which he had been self-confessedly guilty.

In his restitution he went far beyond what was legally necessary. Only if robbery was a deliberate and violent act of destruction was a four-fold restitution necessary (Exodus 22: 1). If it had been ordinary robbery and the original goods were not restorable, double the value had to be repaid (Exodus 22: 4,7). If voluntary confession was made and voluntary restitution offered, the value of the original goods had to be paid, plus one-fifth (Leviticus 6: 5; Numbers 5: 7). Zacchaeus was determined to do far more than the law demanded. He showed by his deeds that he was a changed man.

Dr Boreham has a terrible story. There was a meeting in progress at which several women were giving their testimony. One woman kept grimly silent. She was asked to testify but refused. She was asked why and she answered, 'Four of these women who have just given their testimony owe me money, and I and my family are half-starved because we cannot buy food'.

A testimony is utterly worthless unless it is backed by deeds which guarantee its sincerity. It is not a mere change of words which Jesus Christ demands, but a change in life.

The story ends with the great words – the Son of Man came to seek and to save that which was lost. We must always be careful how we take the meaning of this word *lost*. In the New Testament it does not mean damned or doomed. It simply means *in the wrong place*. A thing is lost when it has got out of its own place into the wrong place; and when we find such a thing, we return it to the place it ought to occupy. A man is lost when he has wandered away from God; and he is found when, once again, he takes his rightful place as an obedient child in the household and the family of his Father.   *Luke 19: 1-10*

ZEALOTS

JOSEPHUS (*Antiquities* 8.1.6.) describes these Zealots – he calls them the fourth party of the Jews: the other three parties were the Pharisees, the Sadducees, and the Essenes. He says that they had 'an inviolable attachment to liberty', and that they said that 'God is to be their ruler and Lord'. They were prepared to face any kind of death for their country, and did not shrink to see their loved ones die in the struggle for freedom. They refused to give to any earthly man the name and the title of king. They had an immovable resolution which would undergo any pain. They were prepared to go the length of secret murder and stealthy assassination to seek to rid their country of foreign rule. They were the patriots *par excellence* among the Jews, the most nationalist of all the nationalists.

The plain fact is that if Simon the Zealot had met Matthew the tax-gatherer anywhere else than in the company of Jesus, he would have stuck a dagger in him. Here is the tremendous truth – that men who hate each other can learn to love each other when they both love Jesus Christ. Too often religion has been a means of dividing men. It was meant to be – and in the presence of the living Jesus it was – a means of bringing together men who, without Christ, were sundered from each other.

Matthew 10: 1-4

ZION

THE temple area covered the top of Mount Zion and was about thirty acres in extent. It was surrounded by great walls which varied on each side, 1300 to 1000 feet in length. There was a wide outer space called *the Court of the Gentiles*. Into it anyone, Jew or Gentile, might come. At the inner edge of the Court of the Gentiles was a low wall with tablets set into it, which said that if a Gentile passed that point the penalty was death.

The next court was called *the Court of the Women*. It was so called because unless women had come actually to offer sacrifice, they might not proceed farther.

Next was *the Court of the Israelites*. In it the congregation gathered on great occasions, and from it the offerings were handed by the worshippers to the priests.

The inmost court was *the Court of the Priests.*

The other important word is *naos,* which means *the Temple proper;* and it was in the Court of the Priests that the Temple stood. The whole area, including all the different Courts, was the sacred precincts (*hieron*). The special building within the Court of the Priests was the Temple (*naos*).

The incident took place in the Court of the Gentiles. Bit by bit the Court of the Gentiles had become almost entirely secularised. It had been meant to be a place of prayer and preparation, but there was in the time of Jesus a commercialised atmosphere of buying and selling which made prayer and meditation impossible. What made it worse was that the business which went on there was sheer exploitation of the pilgrims.

Mark 11: 15-19

PUBLISHER'S NOTE

While all reasonable effort has been made to trace sources of material used within this book, the Publisher would like to apologise if any have been overlooked inadvertantly.

Other books by William Barclay, still in print at the time of going to press, are as follows:

SAINT ANDREW PRESS

SCM PRESS

Barclay Prayer Book 0 334 02460 9
Jesus as they saw Him . . . . 0 334 00800 X
New Testament Words 0 334 01139 6
Gospels and Acts (vol 1) – The First Three Gospels 1 85931 002 8
Gospels and Acts (vol 2) – The Fourth Gospel
  and the Acts of the Apostles 1 85931 003 6

ARTHUR JAMES

William Barclay New Testament 0 85305 288 3
Through the Year with William Barclay:
  Devotional Readings for Every Day – Denis Duncan (ed) 0 85305 252 2
To be re-published
Plain Man's Guide to the Apostle's Creed 0 85305 471 1
Plain Man's Guide to the Lord's Prayer 0 85305 470 3
Plain Man's Guide to the Ten Commandments . . . . 0 85305 472 X

FOUNT PUBLICATIONS

Prayers for Young People 0 00 624580 3
William Barclay Prayer Book – R. Barclay (ed) 0 00 627862 0

FONTANA

More Prayers for the Plain Man 0 00 621110 0

INTERNATIONAL BIBLE READING ASSOCIATION

Introducing the Bible 0 7197 0178 3

MOWBRAY

Testament of Faith 0 264 66377 2

METHODIST CHURCH – HOME MISSION DIVISION

Jesus Christ for Today: Seven Studies in St Luke's Gospel 0 901015 16 4

ABINGDON PRESS

The Master's Men: Character Sketches of the Disciples 0687 23733 5

BIBLE READING FELLOWSHIP

William Barclay Introduces the Bible 0 7459 2279 1

HANDSEL PRESS

William Barclay: Communicator Extraordinary – James Martin . . . . . 1 871828 21 X